Have the Best Year of Your Life

living the breadth of your life
as well as its length

Have the Best Year of Your Life

living the breadth of your life
as well as its length

Jane Matthews

BOOKS

Winchester, UK
Washington, USA

First published by O-Books, 2010
O Books is an imprint of John Hunt Publishing Ltd., The Bothy, Deershot Lodge, Park Lane, Ropley,
Hants, SO24 0BE, UK
office1@o-books.net
www.o-books.com

For distributor details and how to order please visit the 'Ordering' section on our website.

Text copyright: Jane Matthews 2009

ISBN: 978 1 84694 374 4

A CIP catalogue record for this book is available from the British Library.

Design: Stuart Davies

Printed in the UK by CPI Antony Rowe
Printed in the USA by Offset Paperback Mfrs, Inc

We operate a distinctive and ethical publishing philosophy in all
areas of its business, from its global network of authors to
production and worldwide distribution.

CONTENTS

Dedication
For Amy and Paul, who have expanded my life
beyond measure

Acknowledgements

This book grew out of a couple of landmark birthdays. As I hit 49, my sister handed me a box full of shiny envelopes, one for the first day of each month in the coming year. She told me she wanted the months ahead to be spent enjoying new experiences, treats and challenges, rather than contemplating the Big 5-0.

It became, of course, the best year yet; during those 12 months I rode a quad bike, learned to ski again, visited Nuremberg at Christmas and ventured to the theatre to see something other than my usual fare. One month I had a voucher for an enormous bouquet of summer blooms, another, an invitation to choose a piece of art to bring home from a local gallery, and yet another, the chance to revisit with my sister the home we'd spent our first 12 years in. And so it continued: each gift was perfect, but very soon I realized the greater gift was this reminder that we can make any year the best of our lives when we take the time to look up from routine, stretch our comfort zones, reassess the past, and remember to treat ourselves well and our lives as an adventure.

A version of the book in your hands first appeared handwritten in felt pens when it was my sister's turn to be 49. It was my way of gifting to her a year as rich as the one she'd organized for me. Thank you, Shushie, not only for inspiring this book in the first place, but for 'test-driving' it too.

Perhaps it's no coincidence that my 49th year also introduced me to another special person, Patricia Crane, who with her partner Rick trains workshop leaders to share the Heal Your Life, Achieve Your Dreams® philosophy. I'd read and been hugely helped by Louise Hay's book, *You Can Heal Your Life*, but the chance to use the ideas within it to help others on their journey has been life-changing. I continue to learn at least as much from all those who attend my workshops as they do from me, and it is to them, to Louise and to Patricia and Rick that I owe thanks for expanding my life and enriching it through the lessons, tools and themes that underpin much of what you will read.

There are many others, of course, from whose compassionate wisdom I've learned and continue to learn. Their names appear throughout the text and in the recommended reading list at the back, but a special thanks to Susan Jeffers, Dawn Breslin, Lynda Field and Lesley Garner, who gave me permission to quote them at greater length, and to share particular exercises and techniques with you from their work.

During the final stages of putting the book together, when what I most needed was time, space and freedom from worrying about bills, my family stepped up to the mark and made those things possible. Thank you Mum, Tom, and Shushie again, and thank you Amy and Paul for your love and for your faith in me.

Introduction

Welcome to your best year yet.

This is a book like no other on your shelf – one that's going to be your companion for the next 365 days and show you how to have the most exciting, challenging and memorable year of your life so far.

I'm a huge fan of 'self-help' books, and inspiring teachers of personal development tools and techniques: so much so that you'll find me referring to lots of them throughout the coming year.

But, like you I suspect, I've often struggled to stick with all the good advice. Real life has a way of diluting even the best intentions...

Changing habits takes time

If you've ever gone on a crash diet you'll know what I mean. It takes an exceptional human being to change eating habits overnight by sheer force of will.

And there's another reason diets don't usually work. Most are designed only at a superficial level, demanding that we change our behavior without understanding and changing the thinking that lies behind the habits that got us into the fix in the first place.

Inner growth is no different. We don't expect to learn a new language overnight or to take just one driving lesson before heading out onto the highway. We learn and grow best when we allow ourselves time; taking small incremental steps and giving ourselves space to absorb what we've learned, and to embed it into our lives through understanding, familiarity and practice.

I've written this book with those things in mind. To offer you a gentle step-by-step approach to transforming every area of your life. After all, most of us have spent decades learning how to be unhappy or settling for lives of quiet dissatisfaction, stuck in the same habits of thinking and behaving and being. Most of the time we forget we even *have* a choice... if it weren't for that small voice that, in our quietest moments, whispers at us, "are you sure this is as good as it gets?"

Living in the real world

So, no quick fixes. We're going to take our time over this: a year at least, and more if you wish. You've got precisely as long as you need to gently shift the habits that are holding you back and to discover and choose new ones that serve you better. To learn how to bring more peace and pleasure, more fun, excitement and growth into your life: to be the best that you can be.

After all, why rush when, as you'll see, the journey can provide as much joy and richness as reaching the destination, once you begin to use the activities in this book to turn each day into an adventure.

There's another reason I favor taking things gently over the turn-your-life-on-its-head-in-a-week approach. Let's face it, for most of us life is pretty much permanently on fast-forward these days as we juggle a myriad of roles and responsibilities.

Our days are dominated by To Do lists and seemingly relentless demands on our time, energy and purses. Sometimes we wonder where we'll find time to change the sheets, never mind change our lives.

My aim is not to add to your load but to offer you a change program that fits around the realities of your life. Most of the activities in this book can be relatively easily incorporated into any day, and those that take a little extra time or effort can be done on days and at times to suit you. This is *your* best year and you call the shots.

Living the breadth of your life as well as its length

So how are we going to do this? By taking one small step every day. You'll see that this book comprises 52 weeks' worth of exercises, challenges, ideas, growth-work and treats – each activity designed to help you shift a little, to begin to change the habits of your lifetime and discover how rich and rewarding life can be.

You'll find activities that gently expand your comfort zone and give you the chance to try out new things, new thoughts and new ideas. You'll find exercises that allow you to get to know yourself better, to understand how you got to this point in your life, what you want, what brings you alive and how to move beyond that 'automatic' setting that you're so often operating on.

You'll get the chance to inhabit all of you: mind, body, spirit and all six senses - I'm including intuition - and learn how to appreciate yourself more, as well as sharing more love and appreciation with others.

Above all, you'll see how even apparently small changes eventually add up to a big difference. It really is possible to get more out life right now, without waiting for everything to be 'perfect'. The moment that counts is the moment you're in.

All of the activities in this book are about *growth* in some way but to make life simple I've grouped them into seven categories. These seven represent both the key areas where change can take place and, conveniently, the number of days in the week.

That gives you as much flexibility as possible about what you choose to do when. So long as by the end of each week you've tackled something in each area and can congratulate yourself on another seven days of small shifts in a life that counts.

Your best year, a day at a time

These, then, are the seven areas that are our keys to living richer, more joyful and authentic lives:

Grow

Growth is as vital to life as air and water. What doesn't grow stagnates: think of a pond where light can't penetrate. In time, the water darkens and thickens and life can no longer survive. The same is true of our lives when we don't allow light to shine in on them.

At least once a week you're going to get the chance to do just that. The growth exercises are all about getting to know yourself better, understanding how you got the life you have, recognizing thoughts and beliefs that may be holding you back, exploring what you really want and dream of ... on the way to making changes.

So much of the time we are on automatic pilot, hardly aware of the extent to which the things we do, words we speak and choices we make are just habits: habits borrowed from the world we live in rather than discovered for ourselves.

As you begin to understand yourself better through these activities you start to have a real choice about the kind of life you want to create from now on.

Explore

Our world is such a miracle, yet how often do we remember to take the time to notice; to slow down long enough to wonder at the earth coming alive again each spring, or the vastness of an inky night sky? When was the last time you looked beyond your front door and saw the world for what it is: a vast outdoors playground, a place to be an explorer and an adventurer, as well as a reminder that we are part of a timeless cycle of growth, renewal and change? For most of us, that peaceful sense of being just a small part of a bigger miracle left us as we left childhood.

And what about the bodies we inhabit? No matter how we may feel about our shape, weight or appearance, our bodies are the vehicles that move us around and perform thousands of complex biological functions every day without us even needing to think about it.

Our bodies have the most amazing ability to heal and renew themselves and yet so often we treat them like the enemy,

4

disliking them for not measuring up to how we think we should look. So here's a keep fit program that delivers rewards rather than punishment. Each week the explore activities are a chance to really inhabit all of your body, to rediscover the world around you, to reawaken and recharge your senses and tap into that huge capacity for fun, excitement and wonder that we may have lost along the way.

Expand

If you always do what you've always done you'll always get what you've always had.

So often we say we want our lives to change and improve and yet we go on doing the same things in the same way, thinking the same thoughts that we've always thought. Why do we *expect* anything to be different?

Or, to put it another way, what have you got to lose from trying something new?

The expand activities are designed to test the limits of your comfort zone a little and get you in the mood for change. Sometimes it's easier to begin by changing the color of your hair than attempt to change your whole life. Yet as we chip away at lifelong habits, trying new things and old things in new ways, we're re-educating the voice inside that says change is always a risk and we're better off staying put.

Don't worry, I'll be gentle with you while we test those limits you've unconsciously placed around your life, on the way to becoming an expanded version of yourself.

Receive

I'm deliberately telling you about these receive activities before we look at giving; so many of us find receiving harder. And when I write of receiving I don't only mean what others may do for us, but what we are willing to do for ourselves.

One of the biggest challenges facing us in our search for more joyful, loving and authentic lives is learning how to love and appreciate ourselves. The more we practice loving ourselves, the more able we are to love others. The more we appreciate who we are, the more able we are to make good choices. Loving ourselves allow us to create a life based on respect, compassion and truth rather than habit, fear, envy, low self-esteem or any other of the qualities that prevent us achieving our potential and filling the unique place in this world that only we can.

A life full of love and appreciation shines like a beacon for others, and attracts more of both back into our lives.

So forget everything you've been taught about how it's selfish to think about yourself and honor those days in the weeks ahead when I ask you to do something for *you*.

Give
Giving is something you've probably had a lot of practice at.

But in even the most generous of lives there are limits. We may enjoy organizing a child's birthday party or making time to hear a friend's woes but how often are we too preoccupied to notice the parent with a pushchair struggling to get up the stairs? Too busy to pick up the phone or write a letter to a relative who irritates us but who we know is lonely?

Sometimes our kindnesses are conditional on how *we're* feeling, or limited by what we feel comfortable offering. After all, we've been brought up to believe it's important to 'mind our own business'.

It's that belief that often prevents us from taking our place in our communities. Just as a belief that one person can't make a difference stops us taking small actions on big issues like poverty, inequality and the survival of this amazing planet. Whereas the truth is that the biggest moments in history all began with one individual thought or action. Who knows, when we choose to give, where it will lead?

You may find some of the give activities a little challenging,

6

but what they offer you is the chance to rediscover that vital sense of connection and of being a part of something bigger than you are alone. Remembering that as we give to life, so we throw wide the channels for life to give back to us.

Connect

Why do we find it so hard to make time for our lives? Because we've all gone a little mad, creating lives so full of busy-ness and distractions that our heads are always full of noise.

We've become human doings rather than human beings, to whom stillness and peace is so alien we pipe music into our shopping malls and put the TV on 'for company' rather than risk ourselves with silence.

Of all the activities in this book, these connect suggestions are my favorites. For I've learned on my own journey that the most profound insights, guidance and peace come when I allow myself to simply stop.

Each week I'm asking you to do the same: to take a moment to read and ponder a few words of wisdom from some inspiring writers and teachers. To assess whether there is truth in there for you.

It was one of those wise souls who quietly urged us to 'be still and know that every answer you seek lies inside'. We all know so much more than we realize; we've lost sight of the truth that we're the experts on our own lives if we will only take the time to listen to ourselves.

The connect activities are a chance each week to tune into your intuition, inner guidance, heart and soul, where the truth waits.

Commit

In any worthwhile venture there's usually a point when the going gets a little tough: doubts creep in, something knocks our plans for six, or our self-belief starts wobbling.

The word 'commit' has two meanings here. Firstly, I'm asking you to make a commitment to yourself that you'll ride out those doubts and wobbles, even when you can't see results for your effort.

Think of it as like planting a seed and tending it while you wait for it to grow. You can't see what's happening beneath the surface until the day the first green shoots appear to reward your faith.

There will be days when you see the fruits of your efforts, and others when you don't, but a year from now you'll be looking back at a landscape that's changed. You deserve this opportunity to rediscover and recreate a more authentic you. You deserve joy, happiness, peace. You deserve the chance to really live all the days of your life.

And that brings me to the other reason I've called these activities 'commit'. Creating the best lives we can is an ongoing process. I don't believe we ever really stop learning and growing. Nor that we'd want to, when these are the things that make the journey so much more worthwhile.

The commit activities offer you the chance to try out tools and techniques that will serve you long after you reach the final page of this book; for as long as you want to continue moving forward, growing, expanding, exploring, giving, receiving and connecting.

How to use this book

When I wrote the first draft of this book I imagined you picking it up on January 1. New year is traditionally a time when we focus on the ways we want our lives to improve – which may be how you come to have the book in your hands right now.

I'm a fan of anything that helps motivate us, so for those of you who are starting your best year in the new year I wish you a happy and fulfilling new year.

At the same time, one of the most powerful ideas I know is Louise Hay's reminder that *the point of power is always in the present moment.* In other words, every single moment we have the power to make a different choice, to think a different thought: to take control of our lives.

You may have picked this book up on a very ordinary Wednesday in the middle of the year. And if you've done so then something within you knows the moment is right for you to start changing your life.

If that's you then you'll see I've left space each week for you to write in the date so that *your* best year can start the moment you choose.

Why not right now?

You can get anywhere from here

At the start of this introduction I told you I believe small incremental changes are ultimately more powerful in making a real difference. Jump in the car and drive one mile down the road and you are still on familiar territory. But drive one mile a day for 365 days and you'll find yourself somewhere entirely new.

Each of the activities in the book represents one of those miles. So enjoy each one as more distance traveled and remind yourself often of your commitment to go the whole way and see where you end up.

If it really isn't possible for you to do a particular activity then simply repeat one you have enjoyed. But a word of warning here: if your gut is telling you strongly it doesn't want to do something then you need to test that out. Strong reactions often betray an area of our lives we really *do* need to work on

Feel free to swap the activities around to fit with your own life schedule. But be conscious as you do so of being *too* busy. If there is one theme that connects every single activity in this book it's about *making time for your life.*

As for missing a day altogether, well, the sky won't fall down on your head. I promised you a book that you could fit around real life, so let's both accept that there's going to be the odd time when you miss an activity, and days when you have less time, just as there are days when you have more.

What really matters is that when you stumble you don't give up. That's the thing about incremental change: one slip doesn't undo all the good work you've been doing, any more than stopping for a breather on that 365-mile journey will mysteriously catapult you right back to the beginning. It doesn't and it won't.

Just pick up where you left off, or allow your year to be a truly exceptional one that runs for 13 or even 14 months rather than 12! I won't tell!

Share the journey...

There are times when we need the space and quiet that comes from journeying alone, but also times when it helps to have someone to share the view with, to worry about the navigation, to chat to, to moan to and to celebrate with.

For those days when you lack a little motivation, don't want to be alone, or can't wait to share what's happening in your life, then visit the Best Year website, www.bestyear.co.uk. You'll find more ideas and more inspiration there, as well as support with staying the course.

The website is also a chance to catch up on how others are doing with the activities – and to contribute your own ideas, experiences and feedback.

As for those of you who are not fans of computers, do drop me a line via the publishers and let me know how *your* best year is shaping up. I'd love to hear about your discoveries and share in your successes.

May this be not only your best year yet, but the first of many, in an amazing, joyful and fulfilling life that goes on getting better, and better, and better.

With love

Jane

Week 1

date...................

Monday
Explore
Whatever else you may have planned today, make time for a short walk. Living the breadth of your life as well as its length means remembering to climb out of your busy, busy head and be a physical human being too.

As you take your walk, choose one souvenir along the way to bring home and set on your bedside table or kitchen windowsill as a reminder of this, the first day of your big adventure.

On my bookshelf I still have the acorn I brought back from a walk to remind me that the greatest creations start as small seeds.

Tuesday
Commit
This year we're going to be doing some journaling and some activities that will need writing down - quite apart from which I want you to have a record of this amazing year.

So head out today to buy yourself a beautiful notebook in which you can make notes and record what you see, feel, discover, learn and decide.

On the first page, write today's date and a few notes on your hopes and dreams for the year ahead.

Wednesday
Give
Today, leave a book you've really enjoyed in a public place with a note explaining why you love it and want to share it with whoever finds it.

Synchronicity is the word we use to describe those 'coincidences' that happen when the precise thing we need in our lives turns up, whether it's a book that catches our eye, a phone call from someone we've been thinking about, or a car parking spot!

Don't doubt for a moment that your beloved book will fall into the hands of someone who will really appreciate it right now.

Thursday
Expand
There are hundreds of ways in which we stay in our comfort zone every day without giving it a second thought. Yet making small changes to even the most mundane of activities sends a message to ourselves that we are willing to change.

Tonight, flex those change muscles: for one night only, swap sides of the bed. Whether you share your bed with someone (in which case, they're going to get a taste of change too) or tuck up alone, swapping sides gives you the chance to fall asleep and wake up with a very slightly altered view.

Friday
Receive
When you get up this morning, put on a favorite piece of music before you do absolutely anything else. Notice whether starting your day with something you love makes a difference to how you feel.

Saturday
Connect
"Our deepest fear is not that we are inadequate.

Our deepest fear is that we are powerful beyond measure.

It is our light, not our darkness that most frightens us."

In her wonderful book, *A Return to Love*, Marianne Williamson urges us not to 'play small' but to let our light shine.

How about it? As we look ahead to the coming year, are you ready to shine?

Sunday

Grow

Today, let's talk about love, which is a theme we'll be touching on often during the coming year. After all, this book is about creating a life you love.

You're going to get lots of opportunities to look at *who* you love, *what* you love, *how* you love, and how you could love more. But first, let's get straight to the basics by looking at the love you feel for *you*.

Why is it important? Why do we need to learn to love ourselves more?

- because as we grow to love ourselves it becomes much harder to put up with the things in our lives that hurt and damage us;
- because love is an infinitely more powerful springboard for moving forward than fear, anger, guilt or any other of those negative emotions that may lie behind some of the choices we've made up to now;
- because being able to open our hearts to others begins with loving ourselves: just think for a moment how much harder it is to love someone who doesn't love themselves;
- and because, however big a stretch it may be for you to believe this at the moment, you are worth loving.

We'll begin gently with a reminder of why you are worth loving. In your journal write down the names of a few of the people who've loved you and love you still: family, friends, partners, whoever comes to mind. For each of them write a single sentence about what it was or is it that they love about you.

You're allowed to include 'just because', as a reminder that all the time we're busy focusing on our faults and the reasons why we're unlovable, there are people who love us just as we are.

If they can, can you?

Week 2

date....................

Monday
Expand

Just for today, wear jeans into work, for no other reason than the need to shake up your own life a little. If you already wear jeans to work then put on your smartest outfit instead.

Or if your work requires you to wear a uniform, then pin on a badge with a slogan (or wear wildly different underwear from your usual workaday choice).

Tuesday
Connect

Something to think about today:

"There are years that ask questions and years that answer." Zora Neale Hurston

What questions is this year asking you? Are there questions that keep coming up, year after year after year? What are the questions you want to find answers to before we finish this year-long journey together?

Jot down any thoughts in your journal.

Wednesday
Explore

Experience your body fully today. Spend two or three minutes gently stretching everything.

Starting with your feet and toes, flex them, spread them and rotate them, moving up your legs and flexing and stretching the calf and knee muscles. Extend each leg, then, bit by bit, move slowly up through your body, repeating these movements as you focus in turn on each set of muscles. Don't force anything: you're aiming for a soft stretch rather than a tug.

When you've worked around your body try stretching all of

you: stand tall, reach for the sky and feel yourself grow a fraction. You can use this short exercise any time you want to feel more grounded, to move out of your head and into your body, out of your thoughts and into the present moment.

Thursday
Commit

How often do you lie awake at night, turning things over in your mind? Or wake in the night and find it impossible to switch your thoughts off?

Nighttime is for rest, recovery and renewal, which is why one of my favorite tools is the 'daily download', adapted here from Lynda Field's wonderfully practical book *Fast Track to Happiness*.

A bit like running a disk clean-up on a computer, using the daily download helps clear our minds of some of the clutter of daily life. It's also a good way of introducing some of the other key tools we'll soon be practicing such as mindfulness, gratitude and having a positive attitude.

Before you switch out the light, grab your journal and answer the following questions to help you 'park' any concerns, track any growing you've done, and celebrate the richness of the last 24 hours:

1   Today's most significant event was...
2   My main concern is...
3   What I intend to do about that tomorrow is...
4   Something that went better today was...
5   Something I learned today was...
6   Three things that made me smile today were...
7   Things I am grateful for today are...

Do this download regularly and experience the peace of falling asleep with a quiet mind. At the same time you'll be creating a great record of all the growing and discovery you're doing. I find it useful to be able to look back on what I've written, to revisit insights and remind myself how far I've come.

Friday
Receive
Can you remember your favorite meal when you were a child? Cook it tonight.

Saturday
Grow
Last week we started to look at loving ourselves more. One way in which we fail to love ourselves is by focusing on everything that we think is wrong with us; criticizing ourselves for not being good enough, clever enough, beautiful enough, witty enough...enough of anything really.

What's more, we continue with the self-criticism even when it isn't getting us anywhere. Try this exercise:

- in your journal write a list of some of the things you criticize yourself for;
- alongside each item, write down approximately when the criticism started: one year, ten years, half a lifetime?
- taking each item on your list in turn, ask yourself honestly whether criticizing yourself has made a difference. Have you changed anything as a result?

No? I thought not. In which case it's worth considering *what have you got to lose from trying something different?* From making your starting point loving yourself rather than endlessly beating up on yourself?

After all, we know children learn, grow and thrive through love and praise rather than fear and criticism. Isn't that just as true for us?

Sunday
Give

Do something for the community you live in. Pick up litter at a local beauty spot or wash the dirt from a road sign to help others find the way more easily.

Week 3

date....................

Monday
Connect
Something to think about:

"Always be a first-rate version of yourself instead of a second-rate version of somebody else." Judy Garland

We can feel second rate when we're trying to be like everyone else, or endlessly comparing ourselves to others. Are there areas in your life where you're just a pale imitation of someone else? How might you feel, look, act and be different if, instead, you put your energy into being a first rate version of *you*?

Tuesday
Commit
One of the most important themes we'll be working with throughout this year is how in order to change our lives we need to change our thoughts. Many, many people have written and taught about this simple, yet most powerful of all ideas for transforming the way we experience our lives. Among the most accessible, if you want to read more, is Louise Hay's life-changing book *You Can Heal Your Life*.

Think for a moment about how much of your life you live in your head, turning over the things that worry you, frighten you or bring you down. Some may be real; others are just imaginings that may or may not happen.

But what *is* real is that when you have these thoughts you feel bad.

Just as when your thoughts are focused on happy memories, looking forward to things, people you love, you feel good.

It seems our thoughts lead directly to how we feel so why not choose positive ones and feel a little better a little more of the time?

If learning how to feel better isn't enough of an incentive for you, let me also point out that when we're feeling better the rest of our life seems to run better: we feel as if we're 'in the flow', people say yes to us, the things we need turn up, the day-to-day goes smoothly rather than being a struggle.

Best of all, as we come to recognize that changing our thinking changes our lives, we also see, often for the first time, that we are the ones in control. By choosing positive, loving, supportive thoughts we become responsible for our own happiness, our own sense of peace and well-being.

This short exercise will help you to understand the power of our thoughts:

- First, close your eyes and think of something you believe you did wrong, or did badly.
- Remember all the details of it, and notice what feeling it's producing in you. Sit quietly for at least one minute and just let the feeling come.
- Now, as you continue to think about this event or time in your life I want you to think this thought, saying it silently in your head, and allowing yourself to believe it: "I was doing the best I could at the time. I forgive myself. I know I am always doing my best, given the knowledge and understanding that I have."
- Repeat the phrase to yourself several times.
- Then notice how the feeling has changed.

You can use this technique any time you find yourself feeling anxious or upset about something you believe you did or said wrongly.

Wednesday
Give
Why does bad news travel faster than good? From today's newspaper, radio, TV or online news, look out for a happy story

and pass it on to as many people as you can.

Thursday
Expand

Eat something for breakfast that you've never eaten at this time of day before. Whoever said you couldn't start the day with fruit pie or cheese pasta? I once ate custard for breakfast every day for a month when I was traveling, and ever since associate a bowl of custard with new horizons!

Friday
Receive

Remember the joy of receiving pocket money from your parents or relatives, and fantasizing about all the things you might spend it on? When you're turned on by cut-out dolls, comics and cherryade a few pennies can stretch a very long way.

Today, I want you to award *yourself* pocket money: the sort of amount you'd give to a child now. Then spend some time as you once did enjoying planning how you'll spend it: a glossy magazine, a bar of luxury chocolate, a fizzing bath bomb, stink bombs?

The world's your oyster, just as it was way back then.

Saturday
Explore

Make a list of all the places you want to visit under three headings: nearby, striking distance, and far away. Don't stop until you've got at least ten locations down under each heading.

Now put a star against the one you are going to do next. Diary it.

Sunday
Grow

One of the most powerful ways in which we can to learn to love ourselves more is by recognizing the child who still lives inside us.

Often, it's that child who is still waiting to be found out, who worries that he or she doesn't measure up, who sometimes feels lost, lonely, misunderstood, rejected or ignored. Or, when we're feeling really emotional, it may be the child inside who is reacting to old sorrows or challenges: memories that we've buried because we didn't know how to deal with them at the time.

Learning to love ourselves means loving all of the parts of ourselves, including that inner child. And as we do so, it's remarkable how the understanding and compassion we feel seems to carry forward and help us be more loving to our adult selves too.

Try this exercise and you'll see what I mean.

You'll need a little more time than usual, your journal to write in, and somewhere quiet to sit. If possible, find a photo of you as a child to help you go back in time.

Start by spending a few moments studying the picture, looking into your own eyes. (If you don't have a photo, choose a strong memory from your childhood, close your eyes and try to picture yourself as you were in that memory.)

As you look at the picture answer the following questions as if you were still that child:

- What's happening in your life at the moment?
- What do you enjoy?
- Do you have any dreams for the future?
- What are the things that worry you?
- Is anything scaring you?
- What do you need?
- How can I make you happy?

Look over what you've written and ask yourself how you can help that child who still lives inside you now? How many of the things you've written down are still true today?

What can you learn from this exercise about the way you need to treat yourself? Can you start thinking of yourself as someone who needs love and acceptance just as that child did?

You may want to repeat the exercise from time to time, using different photos of you at a range of ages, starting from when you were very young through to those tough teenage years when many of us feel at our most unlovable.

Week 4

date....................

Monday
Explore

Remember a time when strawberries were strictly for the summer and satsumas in the shops meant Christmas was on its way? Life is so much more surprising when we choose to eat what's in season, rediscovering our favorite flavors anew each year. Today, do a bit of homework to find out which foods are in season right now and build them into this week's menus.

Tuesday
Commit

One of the best-known tools for changing our thinking is to use affirmations: powerful statements about what we choose to think.

Believe it or not, you're probably already using them. It's just that for most of us the 'affirmations' circulating in our heads are negative, based on the things we've been taught, or told, or adopted because of the world we live in. Giving them headroom simply reinforces them, until they harden into beliefs about the way things are. *And* make us feel bad.

From now on when I speak about affirmations I'll mean positive thoughts and statements to replace that old negative soundtrack and help shift the way you feel. By writing them and repeating them as though you mean them you are using your conscious mind to re-educate your subconscious.

And, since life has a way of giving back what we give out, as you use affirmations to change how you feel, you start to change the outcomes.

A good example of how this works is going to a job interview. If the thoughts circulating in your head are "I always mess up interviews" and "They won't like me" that's what you'll be communicating to the interviewers.

Whereas if you repeat an affirmation like "I am calm and focused and answer the questions to the best of my ability" *and allow yourself to believe, in that moment, that this is the truth,* you'll feel calmer and better about yourself, and are likely to perform much better. Just ask any of the top athletes or performers who use affirmations to empower themselves before they go 'on stage'.

You can write affirmations for every area of your life and to help you deal with immediate situations. The only 'rules' are that it's helpful to use lively and direct words that bring more energy to your statements. And it's important to write in the present tense, as if these things are true right now.

Repeat your affirmations often, especially at times when your mind is at its quietest and most open; for instance first thing in the morning.

A few of my favorites may help you to get started:

- Every cell in my body is alive with good health
- I easily make time for all the things that matter to me
- Money comes from doing what I love
- I love and approve of the people in my life wholly
- I trust that it is all happening perfectly

Now it's your turn. For today's activity, write one or two affirmations for each of these key areas of your life. Your own words will have more power than mine. Keep them at hand and read, repeat and renew them often:

- Health and wellbeing
- Money and prosperity
- Work
- Love life
- Relationships with others

- Goals and dreams
- Who you are

Wednesday
Connect

"We make a living by what we get, but we make a life by what we give." Winston Churchill

Today, be aware of all the ways in which you are making a life by what you give to others.

Thursday
Give

Wherever you go today, whatever you do, find something to compliment people on.

We've already looked at the critical voice inside our own heads. Criticism is a habit like any other and if we practice it by criticizing others we'll continue to criticize ourselves too.

Cultivating a new habit of noticing what's right about others and ourselves will retrain that carping voice inside our heads.

Go on: there is so much to admire, appreciate and praise in others, and you might just make someone's day...

Friday
Grow

This week we've already talked about using affirmations to help re-educate our internal soundtrack and shift the way we feel inside. Let's continue the theme of learning how to love ourselves by using this wonderfully simple affirmation: I love and approve of myself.

Make it your mantra throughout today, and see how it shifts the way you feel when you say it as though you really mean it.

One day you will.

Saturday
Expand

Today, go to a section of the bookshop or library that you never visit when you're looking for your next read. If you love romance, try science fiction. If you always head for the cookery section, wander over to art or biography.

Your task is to choose something that's the polar opposite of what you normally choose. Who knows, you may even uncover a new passion.

Sunday
Receive

What could you do with 90 minutes today? Vacuum the house? Pull some weeds? Or make yourself a pot of tea, draw the curtains, and snuggle down to watch one of those classic black and white movies from a slower, more mannered and gentle age?

No contest.

Forget the excuses, and take a little time out for you. Old movies are the perfect antidote to our fast-forward world (and it will all still be there when you're ready for re-entry).

Week 5

date....................

Monday
Grow

For today's activity we're staying with the theme of learning to love ourselves, and spending a few minutes seeing ourselves as we really are.

I first came across a version of this exercise in Dawn Breslin's excellent *Guide to Super Confidence*, which is well worth adding to your reading list for this year.

You may have been taught by the world we live in to focus on the negative but deep down is someone with so many fantastic qualities. What's not to love?

I'm going to make this one easy on you by giving you a list of those qualities to help you get started. All *you* have to do is work your way through it and circle *every single word* that applies to you. Ignore the voice that says it's not OK to describe yourself in this way: no one has to see what you've written, except you.

As you work through the list be absolutely honest. This is about who you are at the deepest level: the real you who hides even from themselves.

Adaptable, Adventurous, Attractive, Bright, Calm, Capable, Caring, Committed, Compassionate, Conscientious, Courageous, Creative, Dedicated, Empathetic, Energetic, Friendly, Funny, Generous, Gentle, Hardworking, Honest, Imaginative, Intelligent, Interesting, Intuitive, Kind, Loving, Loyal, Natural, Optimistic, Passionate, Peaceful, Popular, Positive, Powerful, Resourceful, Sensitive, Smart, Sincere, Sympathetic, Talented, Thoughtful, Wise

Now add a few more adjectives of your own and review your list.

Seriously, isn't someone with these qualities worth loving?

If you were describing someone else with these words,

wouldn't you want to be their friend? Wouldn't you love them?

Tuesday
Receive

Treat yourself to a takeout-meal tonight. No cooking. No dishwashing. And you can take your taste buds anywhere in the world you fancy...yum.

Wednesday
Expand

Some people seem to have no trouble airing their views, but many more of us are shy about expressing an opinion. What happens if we get it wrong? What happens if others disagree? Will they stop liking us?

Today, take another small step outside your comfort zone by contributing your views to an internet forum. Choose a subject that interests you and use a search engine to find a forum where people are discussing that topic.

Then, take a deep breath and have your say.

If you don't have a computer, write a letter on a topic you feel strongly about to a newspaper or magazine. Or start a debate with friends or colleagues by asking for their views on something, then offering yours.

Thursday
Connect

"Worrying does not empty tomorrow of its sorrows; it empties today of its strength."

Corrie Ten Boom

To what extent do you undermine yourself and sap your own energy and pleasure in daily life by worrying?

Friday
Commit

If you've been doing the daily download (p. 15) then you're already practicing gratitude.

Gratitude is a powerful tool for two reasons. First, when we take the time to notice what's right in our lives, and how much there is to be thankful for, we're again re-educating our minds to run along a more positive track.

Second, when we're feeling positive, our energy is high and flowing out into the world, opening the way for good things to flow back to us: the more grateful we are, the more we seem to have to be thankful for.

From today onwards, try making gratitude a part of your daily routine. Begin and end each day mentally listing at least 10 things you're grateful for – not just the wonderful things that happen but the abundance we so often take for granted: hot water gushing from the tap, the clean smell of soap, crisp white sheets, a larder full of our favorite foods, a quick hug with a friend, being able to pick up the phone and speak to someone, birdsong, laughing aloud at something on TV, the first sip of a rich coffee, and on and on and on.

Amazing, isn't it, how much we already have to be grateful for when we take the time to pay attention?

Saturday
Give

Write a thank you card to someone who made a difference in your life telling them how, and expressing your gratitude.

Sunday
Explore

When was the last time you skipped? Today, beg, borrow or make a skipping rope and see how many skips you can do without getting tangled up.

Like whistling, skipping is one of those childhood skills we never quite forget how to do, and it's a really fun way to get moving without taking exercise too seriously.

If you're feeling especially brave you might even like to chant a skipping rhyme, or set off skipping down the road like you used to.

Week 6

date....................

Monday
Expand

Today be brave and smile at everyone you meet in the street, especially anyone looking grumpy or cross. Don't worry if you don't get any reaction, or if people respond with bemusement: none of us ever really knows the extent to which the apparently small things we say or do may make a difference in others' lives.

And if smiling at strangers makes you feel uncomfortable, so much the better. That's your comfort zone being stretched again.

Are you getting used to it yet?

Tuesday
Receive

We can't always afford the time or money for a massage so today (and any other day) you can treat yourself to your own gentle touch. Start by closing your eyes, then stroke your forehead lightly, from the center outwards. Next, gently pinch along your eyebrows a few times, then move your fingers down over your temples to stroke your cheeks and lightly tap the delicate skin under your eyes.

Continue by stroking your nose, down onto your upper lip, then softly around your mouth. Then , using the fingers of both hands, apply a soft and stimulating tapping movement all around your face. Finish by running your fingers several times through your hairline (or across your scalp if you have no hair). Feel better?

Wednesday
Connect

Are you ready for one of those Big Questions – the kind of question we sometimes avoid because we're not sure we really want to know the answer?

Coach turned commentator Lou Holtz says: "If you're bored with life – you don't get up every morning with a burning desire to do things – you don't have enough goals."

How do you feel about getting up in the mornings? Is your life in need of one or two new goals? Think about it today.

Thursday
Give
When you go shopping buy an extra tin, packet or portion of one of your favorites and pass it on to a friend or colleague with love.

Friday
Grow
Another way in which we set the bar for loving ourselves too high is when we believe that we have to be perfect.

Have you *ever* met anyone who was perfect? Of course not: we all do the best we can, given where we are in our lives, where we've come from, what we've learned and what we've had to deal with.

How could there be such a thing as perfection when, like fingerprints, we're all uniquely different?

On that note, in your journal write a list of all the ways in which you try to be superwoman or superman. All the ways in which you think you have to be perfect.

When you've done, go back through the list and identify at least two ways in which you can cut yourself some slack. There's a big difference between doing your best and sacrificing your health, happiness and peace of mind on the altar of a mythical perfection that only exists in airbrushed magazines.

Allow yourself to be good enough.

Saturday
Commit

Meditation is a tool we've come to see as something mysterious, surrounded by special ceremonies and rituals, which is a great shame because its benefits are for everyone, from combating stress to getting in touch with our inner wisdom or intuition.

Carving out 10 or 15 minutes a day is like going on a mental holiday to escape from the 60,000 thoughts which scientists say chase themselves around in our heads every day. Meditation is nothing more mysterious than a chance to be still, to quiet our monkey minds and tune into our deepest selves.

If you don't already meditate, then making it a part of your day will bring untold benefits to every area of your life.

- First find a place where you won't be disturbed, whether that means staying 10 minutes longer in bed before the day starts or retreating to the garden shed.
- Experiment with the time of day which seems to benefit you the most, then try to stick to a regular time. The rest are details that you can experiment with: some people like to sit, others to lie down; some find it helpful to have music playing to drown out the everyday sounds of life, others prefer silence.
- What you're aiming to do is stop thinking, to simply 'be' for a short while, and the best technique for achieving this is the one that works for you. There are many methods to try. If this is your first experience of meditation, try the breathing technique to start with: close your mouth and breathe only through your nose. Breathe normally, without effort, but as you do so keep your awareness focused on the flow of air in and out. Follow the cool air entering your nostrils and the warm air coming out. Allow your awareness to flow to and fro with the air.
- Even those who've meditated for years know that

sometimes the mind refuses to be still. If you become aware that you're thinking again just notice the thought and lightly, without beating yourself up, let it go, bringing your attention back to your breathing. All of us have times when we just can't seem to switch off: when that happens remind yourself that even just sitting still for a while is good for body and soul.

As for those times when your mind is truly quiet: savor them. Experience the peace. Sink into that sense of rightness, of stillness, where the authentic you waits; and where all is well.

Sunday
Explore
Remember how at school there was a nature table for all the treasures you and your schoolmates discovered as you explored the great outdoors?

Today, I want you to start your own nature corner: it could be a windowsill, a shelf, or just a bowl in which you can store any treasures that you spot on your outings.

Go in search of a few things to get you started. How clearly I remember the race to be the first to find cattails to bring for the school nature table; exciting proof that spring was on its way.

Week 7

date...................

Monday
Receive

Buy yourself some flowers for your bedroom. It's natural to want to display flowers where others can enjoy them too but these flowers are your treat. So set a vase close to your bed where you can fall asleep and awake to the colors and scents of your own indoor garden.

Tuesday
Expand

Wear your hair in a new style today. If it's always down, put it up. If it's usually up, use tongs to curl ringlets into it or tie it with colored ribbons. If your hair is short, brush it in a different direction, or, if you're feeling especially bold, put a tint in it.

Enjoy the slightly altered face that looks back at you from the mirror. It represents your commitment to change.

Wednesday
Explore

Much of the supermarkets' time and effort goes into developing and introducing new tastes. Yet how often do we really taste the familiar things that appear on our table every day? Time to treat one of our most jaded senses – our sense of taste.

Today I want you to rediscover your appetite for life by making sure you taste everything you eat. No shoving things in your mouth while you hammer away at the computer keyboard or catch up with your favorite TV drama. Stop. Notice. Taste.

And don't stop at familiar flavors. If it's raining, stick your tongue out. Discover what your skin tastes like. Lick the cork or the lid or the spoon. Be adventurous.

Thursday
Grow

Here's another exercise that will help you see the extent to which our thoughts and beliefs create our experience. And how, far from telling it like it is, there are times when our belief that we are not good enough leads us to interpret things in a way that may not even be true.

For instance, as a child we may have been told off for something we did. The adult telling us off was almost certainly motivated by concern for our well-being but what we 'heard' was that we were bad.

Or maybe an important relationship ended and instead of recognizing that the partnership was no longer working, we 'heard' that there was something wrong with *us*.

Right now, I want you to identify two situations where you felt 'not good enough'. Then, taking each situation in turn:

- describe what happened
- recall what message you heard
- and now come up with at least three alternative explanations.

Can you see how choosing a different thought might have made a difference to you?

Friday
Connect

"In this life we cannot always do great things. We can only do small things with great love." Mother Teresa

Today, do every little thing with great love, especially the little things you do for yourself.

Saturday
Give
Clear out a toy cupboard and put everything that's outgrown or no longer needed into a box to take to a local refuge. If you don't have children, donate one or two items from your bookshelf or your larder.

If you don't know where the refuge is, look up support services for domestic violence victims in the phone book, and ask them where you can drop your package.

Sunday
Commit
We've already looked at the way our thoughts influence how we feel, and therefore how we experience the world. The Buddha expressed it even more clearly by saying, "It is our mind that creates our world."

One way of becoming more aware that we need to choose positive thoughts is to ask ourselves the question *if it is my thoughts that shape my life, what kind of thoughts must I have been thinking to create the life I now have?*

Take your journal and answer that question now, looking at the thoughts and beliefs that have played a part in creating what you're now experiencing

- in love
- in your relationships with family and friends
- in your finances
- in your working life
- in your health and well-being
- and in your feelings about yourself.

Are you constantly thinking there's too much to do, telling people you're sooo busy? Guess what, your thinking will continue to attract more busy-ness in your life. Do you expect to be let down in love? Isn't it remarkable how often you are? Do you constantly tell yourself you're overweight? Isn't that just what you've created then?

What we focus on is what we get.

Week 8

date....................

Monday
Receive
Head to your bookshelves or to the library and choose a favorite book to reread and enjoy all over again.

Tuesday
Give
How did you learn to do all the things you take for granted at home, at work, or out and about? Share what you know today by showing someone how to do something: how to use a shortcut on their computer, how to know when fish is fresh, change a plug, play hopscotch, ask the way in French, tie a reef knot. Teaching someone something is a gift that lasts their lifetime.

Wednesday
Connect
Today, sign up to any of the websites that send you a thought for each day. From now on you'll know your morning mailbox is guaranteed to have at least one positive message in it. (If you're not online buy or borrow a book of inspiring quotations and ration yourself to one a day.)

My current favorites are www.thoughtfortoday.org.uk whose daily bites of wisdom are always accompanied by a beautiful picture; and the quirky www.tut.com which is bursting with humor and positivity.

Choose your own favorite from the hundreds you can find on the Internet, and don't be surprised at how often the messages seem to speak directly to something that's going on in your life. We're surrounded by synchronicity once we start to look for it.

Thursday
Grow

Last week we looked at how easily we can turn situations, and other people's behavior, against ourselves. Today, I want you to build on that by learning how not to take it personally.

Sometimes it's about us; more often it's really not. Trust me, we've just got into this damaging habit of interpreting every single negative as more evidence of what is wrong with us.

Throughout the day, practice *not* taking it personally by deflecting any negative that appears to be coming your way. Whenever anyone says or does something that seems to be directed at you then quietly and deliberately *turn it around in your head*:

- He's not angry with me. He's just angry.
- She's not upset with me. She's just upset.
- They're not disappointed in me. They're just disappointed.

Maybe there are things you could have done better; perhaps you did make a mistake – or not.

Using this technique helps to take the emotion out of your reaction, which, in turn, enables you to respond calmly, or not respond at all. Rather than adding your hurt feelings to what's already out there, like fuel to a fire.

Who knows, as you practice this technique, in time you may even come to see that it's only about you if you allow it to be.

Friday
Commit

How has your meditation practice been going?

Hopefully you've been making the time to be still, but if not, don't worry: eight weeks into this year of discovery you must surely know that we can *always* choose to begin again at any moment.

An alternative to the breathing meditation we've already looked at is mantra meditation. A mantra is just a word or phrase you repeat quietly in your head over and over in order to focus your attention inwards, away from the thoughts that usually run riot in your head.

You can use any word or sound, or choose according to your mood or circumstances. For instance, at times of stress I like to meditate with the mantra 'I am' (on the in-breath) 'relaxed' (on the out-breath). Other words people like to use include 'love', 'peace', 'shanti' (meaning inner peace), or sounds such as 'ohm' or 'aum'. As you practice more, and begin to really enjoy your meditation sessions, there are so many different mantras and techniques to try.

The best is the one that works for you.

Saturday
Explore
"When you get the chance to sit it out or dance...I hope you dance."

Play Lee Ann Womack's inspiring song, or any other music you love to move to. Shut the door on your private moment and really go for it, flow with it, and allow the music to move you where it wants.

No one is watching and your body will truly thank you for it.

Sunday
Expand
You've already been a teacher this week; now it's time to be a student. After all, expanding our lives means gently stretching every bit of us, including our brains.

Identify one area of your knowledge or expertise – a hobby, something connected to your profession, or just general knowledge – then find something new on this topic to read and learn.

Week 9

date....................

Monday
Give

Leave a silver or gold-colored coin where a child will find it.

Tuesday
Grow

Another of those big questions for you today. Without thinking about it, in your journal quickly write down your answers to the following two questions. (Writing quickly makes it harder for the 'yes buts' to pop up and try and censor or argue with what you want to write.)

- If I really loved myself I would...
- If I really loved myself I wouldn't...

Keep your answers safe and look back on them often: they are your blueprint for a more loving life.

Wednesday
Connect

"If you want to know what your thoughts were like yesterday then check how your body feels today." Indian proverb

The way we feel is a sure-fire clue to the kind of thoughts we've been giving headroom to.

How are you feeling today?

Thursday
Receive

Go online or get on the phone and order yourself something luxurious to arrive by mail: bath products, jewelry, a new book by your favorite author. It's such a buzz when the postman knocks at your door with a package.

Friday
Expand
Today, go somewhere for lunch that you've never tried before: a new restaurant, a working man's cafe, a soup bar. You could even just take a pack of sandwiches (with a new filling!) to a park you've never visited.

Saturday
Commit
Let me ask you something: what was the first thing you noticed when you woke up today? Can you name three smells you've been aware of since waking? What about sounds: did you notice the birds this morning? Or the color of the sky?

Or was it all just background?

For many of us it's usually about getting *through* the day, rather than being *in* the day. We're either chewing over something that's happened or planning what we'll do next. Living in the past, or the future; almost never in the present.

And yet, as Eckhart Tolle points out in his book *The Power of Now,* the present, the now, is the only moment that really exists.

To get more out of life we need to be more present in our lives; to experience more moments in the now. One way of doing this is to practice mindfulness.

If you want an example of what mindfulness feels like, think back to your last holiday. As you slowed down, broke with daily routine, tried new things, looked out over the unfamiliar, didn't your senses all seem to be heightened – a bit like stepping out of a black and white movie into a Technicolor film?

Didn't you feel more alive than you'd felt for months?

For your first exercise in mindfulness, think back to the last time that you really did feel truly alive: so alive that time seemed stretched, maybe even halted.

Now, ask yourself, what were the ingredients that enabled you to truly experience life in all its dimensions for those few minutes, or hours, or even days? What was different about you, your attitude, your thoughts, and what was different about the way you were living?

In your journal write a few notes on anything that this small exercise teaches you about things you can do to bring more of those 'alive' moments into your daily life?

Sunday
Explore
Another way of bringing nature into our homes is to use a kitchen wipe-off board or whiteboard to keep track of the changing seasons. No matter when you're reading this, start to keep a note of any sign that the year is slipping into the next season. Have you got an irresistible urge to clean out the cupboards or have you just seen the first lambs? Then spring's on its way. Does the morning air smell damp and rich? Autumn is just around the corner.

Recording signs of the turning seasons not only anchors us in the present moment; it's a great reminder that we too are part of the natural world, our moods and energies responding to the changes happening just beyond the backdoor.

Week 10

date....................

Monday
Connect

"The genius of life is to carry the spirit of childhood into old age." Aldous Huxley

What characteristics of childhood would help you get more out of life now? Curiosity, trust, playfulness, freedom, a sense of wonder?

Write your own list.

Tuesday
Give

Sometimes it feels like a battle zone out there, with people treating their cars like weapons, channeling their anger, fears and frustration through their arms and legs into the way they drive.

Be a peacemaker on the roads today by letting people pull out in front of you in traffic, smiling at the other drivers when you're waiting at the lights, traveling with care and attention to everyone else on the road. Honestly, those small kindnesses will make a difference to others, whatever kind of day they're having.

If you don't drive, step aside for people in the street or let others get onto the bus ahead of you. Be a peaceful traveler.

Wednesday
Commit

In case you were wondering, the opposite of mindfulness is multitasking, trying to juggle a dozen different tasks at the same time without dropping any of them.

Imagine the strain we put ourselves under: no wonder multitasking has been described as a curse rather than a skill.

One way to free us from the tyranny of too many tasks, and

remind ourselves to practice mindfulness, is to *do one thing at a time.*

Start by writing a To Do list so you don't need to worry about forgetting something. But once you've done so, set it aside and consult it *only* each time you complete the task you've chosen to tackle.

If you're doing this at work, the same applies to email and the phone: you're only allowed to check them between tasks; not while you're engaged on something else.

I promise you, it will all still get done.

The difference is that you'll gain a whole lot more satisfaction from everything you do, *and* be more present in your life while you're doing it.

Thursday
Grow

If there's one area of our lives where the human race has got truly mixed up it's in our emotional lives. The fact that calling someone 'emotionless' or 'too emotional' are both considered criticisms shows how confused we are about what to do with our emotions.

As a result, we've had very little training in how to handle and express our emotions. Either we expend a huge amount of energy keeping the lid on them or we let them control us, expressing them in ways that damage ourselves and others, a bit like the mess that results from trying to keep the lid on a boiling saucepan.

If you think about it, denying our emotions, keeping them hidden, is denying a part of ourselves. Deep down we're saying *we're* not acceptable because we feel these horrible things.

Not only does that make it much harder to practice love and acceptance for ourselves, it also diverts energy that we could be putting into more positive things.

In the coming weeks we'll shine a compassionate light on a few of those difficult emotions but today I'd like you just to jot down a few thoughts in your journal on which emotions you consider 'unacceptable'.

What do you remember about seeing people being emotional when you were growing up? How about when you were emotional yourself – what happened? How do you feel now when someone gets emotional around you?

Friday
Explore
Tune into the soundtrack of your life today by creating a sound map. Find a place to sit outdoors, in your backyard, at the park, the town center, or even indoors if it's a wet day.

Take a piece of paper and pens or pencils and draw yourself at the center of the map. Now add in little pictures to represent all the sounds you can hear.

Put them on your drawing where they are in relation to you and in relation to each other. Choose a fun way to represent each sound, so, for instance, a cooing dove might appear as a beak on your sound map, while the ring of a mobile phone might look like musical notes.

It's amazing, the sheer richness and volume of the soundtrack that is played out around us every day. Yet how often do we stop and really listen?

Here's your chance.

Saturday
Receive
Paint, crayon or collage a rainbow and stick it into your journal or on the wall. Let it remind you that even on the dull days we're surrounded by beauty if only we take the time to stop and notice.

Sunday
Expand
Singing is a wonderful way of literally expanding, opening up

our lungs and ourselves – as long as we're not worried about anyone hearing us. Find your voice and open up today by singing to your favorite music as you get ready to leave the house, as you cook, make the beds or wash the dishes. Sing in the bath or shower, and to your reflection in the mirror.

Week 11

date....................

Monday
Commit

We all need to learn how to slow ourselves down and relax when life is threatening to get on top of us.

This relaxing breath, described by Dr Andrew Weil on his excellent CDs *Breathing: The Master Key to Self Healing,* is a really effective way of stopping the world for a moment.

Here's how:

- Rest the tip of your tongue lightly behind your front teeth.
- Breathe out through your mouth making a whooshing sound.
- Close your mouth and breathe in through your nose to the count of four (to help you count at the right speed use the word 'potato' after each number: one potato, two potato, three potato, and so on.
- Hold your breath lightly to the count of seven.
- Then exhale through your mouth, lips slightly pursed, to the count of eight.

The power of this technique comes from the lengthy out-breath, which forces the body to take in a much greater volume of air on the in-breath. Most of the time we breathe so shallowly, especially when we're stressed.

The more often you practice this one, the easier it will become but don't do more than four sequences at a time and stop if you feel lightheaded.

If you're interested in adding a few more breathing techniques to your toolkit, try www.drweil.com.

Tuesday
Explore

We're far better at noticing unpleasant smells than those that delight us or trigger a happy thought or memory. Today, go in search of smells that make you smile: freshly ground coffee, clean skin, coconut perfume coming from a travel agent's, baby powder, cut grass. Consciously seek out wonderful smells and, as you do, breath deeply, giving your nose a treat and a workout.

Wednesday
Receive

Invent your own smoothie to enjoy today. Mix a selection of fruits or vegetables with a splash of juice and blend to a smooth liquid. It's a lovely chance to experiment and, as you take your first slurp, think how grateful your body will be for this burst of vitamins, minerals and other goodies. A tip: if you opt for vegetables, adding a splash of lemon juice and chopped cucumber adds a real zing to your drink.

Thursday
Connect

Something to think about:

"My imperfections and failures are as much a blessing from God as my successes and my talents." Mahatma Gandhi

Think of the ways in which what you see as your failures and imperfections have given you opportunities for learning and growth – as well as allowing you to show compassion and empathy for others

Friday
Give

Send a 'wish you were here' postcard of your home area to a friend or family member who you haven't seen for a while. Getting post for no particular reason is the best post of all.

Saturday
Expand

Can you remember what you used to enjoy doing as a child? Isn't it amazing how we give up on so many pleasures, for fear people will think we're being 'childish'?

Today, think of being childish as a compliment, and rediscover one of your favorite childhood pursuits. See how high you can swing at the park, jump in a puddle without worrying about the laundry, make and serve a mud pie or concoct your own perfume from rose petals.

Sunday
Grow

One of the toughest emotions to deal with is anger. Thinking back to what you wrote last week about emotions, do you have a healthy attitude to anger, do you stuff it down, or do you get angry inappropriately or out of proportion to what's gone on?

One of the most important things to know about anger is that it's a very physical emotion and needs a physical outlet. For today's exercise, you're going to begin to express any anger physically through a pen and paper. Give yourself at least four minutes to answer this question as many times as you need to:

- I am angry with (their name) for... (what's your anger about?)

It may be you're angry with lots of people, or the same people over and over. Let it all spill out of you without any censorship (you can tear up or burn your paper later) and use as many underlinings and exclamation marks as you need to really vent.

Giving yourself permission to express what's been festering inside is the first, courageous step in opening the wound in order to be able to clean it out and start the healing process.

In some cases, just the act of acknowledging to yourself that you're angry may be enough to free you up.

Other angers go much deeper and may require a great deal more work and attention. That might involve taking some action or talking to whoever it is you're angry with, but before you make any decisions you first need to take more heat from your anger by being even more physical.

Below, are just a few suggestions for other ways in which, from now on, you can find an outlet for the worst of your anger *before* you do anything that could hurt you or others. Remember, however much cause you have for being angry, you're the one who's hurt the most by hanging onto emotions that block you.

- *Write a letter:* Grab a piece of paper and onto it pour out all the fury you want to direct at whoever or whatever has made you angry. Use a big black or red felt pen with lots of capital letters. Write as quickly as you can. And when you've finished, tear it into tiny pieces.
- *Have a smashing time:* Next time you're at a car boot or yard sale pick up a pile of old plates and mugs. There is nothing to beat the release that the sound of breaking china brings. Make sure you can hurl it safely: down the end of the garden or in the garage with the doors shut. When your anger is spent grab the broom or dustpan and brush. Sweeping up is physical too, and almost as therapeutic.
- *Power your way to peace:* Go for a five-minute power walk, slamming the door behind you. Walk as though you are competing for an Olympic medal. Allow the anger to flow right through your arms and legs as you swing them furiously from side to side, covering the ground in huge steps. If you're at work or home and can't get away, then do a few laps of the building or march up and downstairs 20 times.
- *Sock it to your sock drawer:* Every time you rip a pair of stockings or put a hole in your socks, stuff them into an old

pillow case rather than throwing them away. You'll soon have loads, and a home-made punch bag that hurts a lot less than the ones the boxers use. You could hang it from a joist in the garage or garden shed. Or simply stuff it under the bed to be yanked out and pummeled in an anger-emergency.

Week 12

date...................

Monday
Connect

Louise Hay points out that, " Since time began on this planet, there have never been two snowflakes alike or two raindrops the same. We are meant to be different... when we can accept this, then there is no competition and no comparison."

To what extent do you give yourself a hard time by trying to be like other people? To look like them, behave like them, want the same things as them?

Turn that on its head today by reminding yourself often that the only person you have to be is the person who is uniquely you. We're *meant* to be different or we wouldn't have been created that way.

Tuesday
Expand

Eat at least one meal today with nothing but your food and yourself for company. That means no reading or watching TV. No company to distract you. Just a chance to pay attention to what you're doing and really taste what you're putting into your mouth for a change.

Wednesday
Grow

One reason we hide our emotions is because we feel guilty for having them in the first place. Many years ago I was a carer for a relative who never seemed to notice that caring for him had turned my whole life on its head. I was running myself ragged, trying to juggle the responsibilities of caregiving, family, home and work.

What made all this harder was feeling resentful – and trying to stuff those feelings down because I didn't like what they said about me. What sort of person resents someone who's dying of cancer for not appreciating them more?

Once again, such emotions grow more powerful so long as we keep them buried, hidden even from ourselves. Learning to love and approve of ourselves means accepting that we are the way we are. Rather than being scared of those darker emotions we can treat them as signals, warning lights on a dashboard that show us something is wrong and needs to be addressed.

In truth, my feelings of resentment were understandable. And by acknowledging them I was able to recognize that I needed to make changes in how I cared for my relative for the sake of my own sanity.

Our responsibility begins and ends with what we choose to *do* with our difficult feelings. Feeling resentment isn't wrong: expressing it by taking it out on whoever happens to be standing close by is.

Today, look at whether you're feeling resentful of anything or anyone.

- Complete the sentence I am feeling resentful about...(what?) or I am feeling resentful with...(who?) as many times as you need to.

This week take dealing with difficult emotions a step further by looking at each statement you've written in turn and answering the questions:

- what lies behind this feeling?
- what if anything do I need to do about it?

Thursday
Commit
How are you doing with those niggling negative thoughts? Are

you learning to spot them and replace them with thoughts that feel better or with affirmations? Are you regularly asking yourself how you're feeling so you can work out what sort of thoughts you've been having?

Or does changing your internal soundtrack feel like a mountain to climb?

Fear not, any habit takes time to change and you've got precisely as long as you need.

Meantime, another technique you may find helpful in pricking the power of negative thoughts is humor.

When I catch my mind grumbling on in its old familiar negative way, I repeat the thought aloud but in my squeakiest cartoon voice, gently poking fun at myself.

Another effective technique is to be overly dramatic and say something like "out, ridiculous thought!" in your best stage voice.

Today, experiment and see what brings a smile to your face and lightens your heart as the negativity dissolves.

Repeat after me: "I choose thoughts that make me feel good."

Friday
Give

Even if you're not a church-goer, churches and religious centers have a special atmosphere where believers and non-believers alike may find peace, reassurance, consolation, and relief from their troubles.

Today, find a church and light a candle for someone who needs warmth and hope in their lives right now.

If you can't get to a church or religious center, or don't feel comfortable with the idea, set a lighted candle in your window instead and spend a few moments imagining love beaming out from the flickering flame to whoever needs it.

Saturday
Receive

Treat yourself to a manicure today. Loving and taking better care of ourselves extends even to our extremities.

You can either adventure down to the nail bar in town and choose from all those fantastic colors and designs (in which case today's activity could also count as an 'expand'). Or lock yourself in the bathroom with some lovely music to listen to while you shape, buff, polish and paint your fingers or toes – or both – in a color that makes you smile with pleasure.

Sunday
Explore

Today get some bubble mix or dilute a capful of dishwashing liquid, and blow bubbles to your heart's content. How big can you blow? How many bubbles can you create with a single breath? What's the longest time they last? How many colors can you see in them?

Week 13

date....................

Monday
Expand
Today, do something naughty.

Tuesday
Explore
"For everything there is a time and a place."

Today, I want you to become aware of your body's natural rhythms.

These days, we often have to fit our lives around someone else's timetable, at work and at home.

But that needn't stop you learning more about your body rhythms, becoming aware of your energy highs and lows; when you feel at your brightest and best; when you'd rather stop or fade out for a while; when you dip and when you soar.

Understanding the natural ebb and flow of our personal energy is a useful starting point for making choices to ease life along a little more smoothly. If you're at your most productive at the crack of dawn, why fritter that time away on household chores, or sleeping late in bed?

Conversely, once you identify the times that your body wants to rest and recuperate, you can try and be kinder to yourself then, maybe building your break or quiet times around them, rather than forcing yourself to 'push through'.

Wednesday
Commit
Focusing again on gratitude, and all the ways in which our lives do work and are already abundant, today write a list of all the people you have a reason to be thankful for, and why you are grateful to them. Start with the people who've made a difference,

helped you, taught you something, been there for you, or brought love, laughter, joy and companionship into your life.

Thursday
Connect

Remember what I wrote in the introduction to this book - if you always do what you've always done, you'll always get what you've always had?

This whole book is about making small changes and there's the reason why. It's said that the definition of insanity is to go on doing the same thing day after day and expect that somehow, one day, the outcome will be different.

Today, think about how that applies in *your* life. How much of the time are you doing, saying, thinking, reacting, believing and expecting in exactly the same way you did yesterday, and the day before, and the day before that?

Consider the possibility of changing one thing at a time in order to change your whole life.

Friday
Receive

How often do you get your best things out, or, like me, do you squirrel stuff away in cupboards and only remember to use it when there's a 'z' in the month?

Today I want you to use your best china...and your crystal glasses...and your poshest tablecloth, even if you're only having baked beans on toast and juice for supper.

It's actually really simple to turn an 'ordinary' day into something a little special. Bringing out the best things is a reminder we can make absolutely any day special the moment we remember we can choose to do so.

Saturday
Grow

We touched on feeling guilty last week: guilt is both a response to some of those 'unacceptable' feelings, but also a difficult emotion in its own right. We all suffer from it: guilt for things we did or didn't do, no matter that they might have happened decades ago.

But just like anger, resentment, envy and other difficult emotions, unacknowledged guilt can block us, and knock us off the path of authenticity. For instance, have you ever done something you really didn't want to do because you felt guilty?

This week, let's expose your guilty feelings to the healing light of day. In your journal record the words, deeds and events you still feel guilty about.

As you bring them out into the open, remind yourself that you're no better or worse than anyone else: we all have skeletons in our cupboards. But so long as we keep things hidden from ourselves, we give them power in our sub-conscience. Once we know what we're dealing with we can consider forgiving ourselves in order to be able to move on.

Sunday
Give

Are you like me, keeping a few small gifts in reserve for those panicky moments when you realize you've forgotten someone's special day and need to get something to them quickly? Today's gift is a little like that: something you may never need but important to keep in reserve, just in case.

I'm talking about learning how to give the kiss of life, mouth to mouth resuscitation, artificial respiration.

There are plenty of places where you can pick up the basics, from first aid manuals and homecare books, through any number of websites such as the Red Cross', to classes.

Take the time to learn what to do. You'll probably never need to use it, but just imagine how much this gift would mean should the day ever come that you do.

Week 14

date...................

Monday
Give
Today include notes in everyone's lunchbox, or slip a loving message into someone's pocket. How about: 'I am so proud of you and grateful to have you in my life'.

Tuesday
Expand
Today, write a letter or send an email to your local MP, government representative, or to the Prime Minister or President, on a subject you feel passionately about. Tell them what you want them to do, ask them to act and to report back to you. Remember, it's their job to represent your views.

Wednesday
Connect
According to Wayne Dyer, "It is a simple procedure to calculate the number of seeds in an apple. But who among us can ever say how many apples are in a seed?"

This is a wonderful way of expressing the truth that we can never know what we seed in others' lives. How something relatively small may one day produce a whole orchard.

Today, ponder on and celebrate the unseen, unknown difference you've made, and continue to make, in the lives of family, friends, acquaintances and those you may never even meet.

Thursday
Commit
If you haven't already tried it, use music to meditate to today. A softly repetitive sound can help lull our busy minds into a more

relaxed state, while inspiring music can take us deeper into a meditative state, to the center of ourselves.

My personal favorites are *Angel Love* by Aeoliah and Jenny James' *Sleeping Angels*, but I also use CDs with only the sound of the waves, a forest stream, or the dawn chorus.

There are so many choices on the shelves of your local bookstore, or on the Internet. Have fun seeing what works for you.

Friday
Grow

In the past few weeks we've been looking at the difficult emotions that may be blocking us: anger, resentment and the guilt we feel towards ourselves and others.

But there comes a time when, in order to move forward, we have to be willing to leave stale emotional baggage behind.

Forgiveness is a gift we give ourselves. It may not be able to alter what's happened in the past but it *can* expand the future.

Just imagine for a moment how we handicap ourselves when we insist on dragging half a lifetime's stuff along with us. Forgiving the past is such an important part of lightening our own load: freeing us up, unlocking our hearts in order to be able to express and grow through more positive emotions and feelings.

Learning to forgive is learning how to let go. Leaving the bags where they are or, if that's too big a stretch for you right away, imagining you're checking them into left-luggage, so you can choose whether or not to go back for them one day.

- Today, spend a little time writing in your journal about those you need to forgive. Who are the people who have hurt you? Disappointed you? Let you down?
- Are there things you need to forgive yourself for?

It may help to look back at what you wrote about the people you're angry with and the reasons you feel guilty.

Then think about how you will forgive them. It can be powerful to write your forgiveness in the form of a letter, for your eyes only, explaining what you are forgiving each person for. Or you may prefer to speak it aloud, finding somewhere private where you can express your forgiveness as though they were in the room.

Don't expect to turn every difficult feeling on its head in a single session. But do congratulate yourself for beginning the work of forgiving those you need to, knowing you can return to this exercise any time and that each time you do so, the one who gains the most is you.

Saturday
Explore
You'll know the expression 'to stretch your legs' but do you know how it feels to do it?

Absolutely fabulous!

Today, instead of sauntering or sleepwalking try properly stretching your legs. Whether you take yourself out on a walk, or simply practice stretching your legs as you're moving around the office or up and down the stairs of your home, the important thing is to pay attention to them. Try making your stride a fraction longer than usual; feel the muscles working, the joints smoothly setting you in motion, and the energy powering you forward.

Now *that's* stretching your legs.

Sunday
Receive
Write a short wish-list: three categories representing what you would like to have, to do and to be. Note down at least ten items in each category.

There'll be at least one thing on your list that you can make happen now. Do so.

Week 15
date....................

Monday
Explore
Borrow a bird book from your local library or visit a bird or wildlife charity's website and learn how to identify three or four of the most common birds you may spot in your garden, local park, or hovering over the grass verge as you race down the highway. It's lovely to be able to put a name to the things we so often take for granted.

Tuesday
Connect
"Yes, there is nirvana; it is in leading your sheep to a green pasture, and in putting your child to sleep and in writing the last line of your poem." Kahlil Gibran

Can you describe your 'nirvana' in such simple and true terms?

Wednesday
Give
Bake a cake to take into work or to give to a friend or neighbor. Cakes are for special days, so make this one!

Thursday
Grow
Learning to recognize and handle our emotions wouldn't be complete without a look at one of the most damaging of all: fear.

It's natural to be scared when we're facing something dangerous. Fear can keep us safe from harm.

But how many of us also feel fear when we're simply facing something new, or unusual, or that might take us out of our comfort zone?

At such times, instead of keeping us safe fear keeps us stuck. What's more, such fear is often not real but exists purely in our imaginations, rather like the way we feel watching a scary film.

All the 'what ifs' that haunt us as we wonder what might happen if we dare move home, change jobs, end the relationship, speak up for ourselves. We can't *know* what will happen: it may go well, it may not, but we scare ourselves silly anyway.

Why do you think film-makers keep the scary thing hidden as long as possible? Once we see what's been frightening us the reality is rarely as fearful as we imagined. Just like the movies, as we find the courage to name our fears so we take away some of their power over us.

Today, begin the work of shining some light on your shadows. On a piece of paper write down what it is you're scared of, from relatively small fears such as being scared of creepy crawlies to those really big ones like getting sick or something happening to someone you love.

As you name each of your demons, remind yourself they may or may not be real. We'll be returning to that list next week so for now keep it safe.

Friday
Commit

The past may be 'another country' but our experiences there have shaped where we are now. Our memories and experiences are our foundation stones, for good or ill, and excavating them can help us decide what to keep, what to shed, and where we may need to create new foundations.

Today, begin your explorations by writing a brief version of your life story.

There are a number of ways to do this, depending on how much time you have and whether your mind prefers to work chronologically, or on themes.

For example, you could go through year by year writing one line for each, recalling where you were, what you were doing and how you were feeling.

Or, using graph paper, try drawing your life as a timeline of peaks and troughs and flats, jotting a few words of explanation about what lies behind the position of the line as you go.

If you have less time, you could be selective and describe your life as it was in each decade. For instance, write a paragraph about yourself and what your life looked like when you were aged 9, 19, 29, 39 and so on up to the last birthday with a 9 in it.

Or write a paragraph about your life journey in each of a number of key areas: family, love, home, work, life purpose, friends and so on.

Do this in your journal where you can return to your story and write more throughout this year as we begin to identify the things that have shaped you and the patterns in your life.

Saturday
Receive

Why is it that as children we'll do anything to resist being sent for a nap, yet as adults, however much we'd love to creep away and lie down for a few minutes, we don't allow ourselves to?

Today you can. Head for your bed (or a bench if you're not at home) in the early afternoon, pull the covers up to your chin, breathe in the cozy smell of your sanctuary and close your eyes for a short spell.

Set the alarm if you're worried about overdoing it. Or, lie on top of the covers and tell yourself it's a power nap if you're struggling to do this small thing for yourself.

I find it works best when I keep the nap short. And I promise you the world won't go anywhere while you're allowing yourself to step off for a few sweet moments.

Sunday
Expand

Get a map and draw a circle around your home that extends approximately 12 miles. Now look inside the circle for a place you've never been. It could be a museum in another town, a tiny village you've always bypassed, a public park or gardens; whatever catches your eye.

Now go and pay a visit. It's so easy to overlook what's right under our noses. By becoming a tourist in your own backyard, you're once again practicing mindfulness.

Week 16

date....................

Monday
Commit

Last week you tried to capture the headlines of your life story up to now. Today, let's continue our excavations by looking at friendship.

In your journal write about the best friend you had when you were growing up. Describe why the friendship was important. And consider whether you still need any of the same things from your friendships today.

Are you still the same sort of friend to others as you were then?

Tuesday
Connect

Something to think about – and to commit to memory today:

HALT is a technique taught by the wise people at Alcoholics Anonymous to prevent us being the victims of our feelings.

The letters are a reminder that whenever we're feeling Hungry, Angry, Lonely or Tired, we need to deal with that first before doing anything else. Especially if that something else involves other people, making decisions or tackling something challenging.

How often do you sabotage yourself by choosing to start a difficult conversation when you're tired or hungry? Or carry your anger about a situation into something entirely unrelated?

Wednesday
Receive

Treat yourself to a face mask today, either a ready-prepared one, or whip up your own using yogurt and oatmeal and cucumber slices for your eyes.

(Let me share a secret – the mask is actually less important than the five minutes you're going to have to sit and do nothing while the mask is working. Enjoy!)

Thursday
Expand
Today, open that cookbook you haven't used since you were first seduced by its wonderful pictures, and choose a recipe to try out. Don't be put off by a long list of ingredients, or by names of ingredients you've not heard of. The more different this one is from the way you usually approach cooking, the more that comfort zone around you is stretching.

Friday
Give
Today, take a plant, a bunch of flowers, or some new magazines to a local nursing home or hospital and ask the staff to pass them on to someone who doesn't get many visitors.

Saturday
Explore
This week, see the dawn.

Chances are by the time you read this it may be too late to watch the world wake up today, so make a plan to do so sometime this week. Set your alarm clock to ring early, make yourself a hot drink, wrap yourself in a blanket and find a spot outdoors to enjoy the spectacle: the cries of the first birds, the dusting of lighter sky on the horizon, the still air of a new morning.

Pure magic – and it's there for the taking every single day.

Sunday
Grow
According to Susan Jeffers, author of the unmissable *Feel the Fear*

and Do It Anyway®, there is one thing lying behind all our fears, and that's the belief that we won't be able to handle it. Redundancy, illness, disappointment, rejection, bereavement: we're afraid we'll fall apart.

Today, spend a few quiet minutes writing in your journal about the times when your worst fears *were* realized. When you got the sack, a loved one died, you got dumped, you had no money to meet the unexpected bill, you got hurt.

Now, as you recall each of them, remind yourself that you did handle those things somehow. You wouldn't be here if you hadn't.

Battered, bruised, but still a survivor.

Week 17

date....................

Monday
Receive

After yesterday's courage in remembering those times when your worst fears were realized, you deserve a reward. Take time out to visit your favorite coffee shop, alone or with friends, for a relaxing drink and a sticky bun.

Tuesday
Commit

Have you done the daily download (p. 15) lately. Healthy habits take time to get established so if you haven't remembered to allow yourself those few minutes to reflect on the last 24 hours then do so tonight. And tomorrow?

Wednesday
Give

Buy something from a vending machine but leave it in the drop zone for the next person to find and enjoy as an unexpected bonus.

Thursday
Connect

Something to think about today:

"One word frees us of all the weight and pain of life: that word is love." Sophocles

How could you love more?

Friday
Grow

So, what are the ways in which fear is cramping *your* style or stopping you from moving in the direction of your dreams?

In *Feel the Fear and Do It Anyway®*, Susan Jeffers suggests we use the affirmation "Whatever happens, I'll handle it", to help us face our fears and move through them.

As we discovered last week, it's unlikely any of us will get through life without losing someone we love, without a love affair ending, without finding a hole in our finances. But, as you contemplate those areas of your life where fear may be holding you back, ask yourself in which frame of mind you're more likely to succeed: the one in which a little voice is whispering, "What if it all goes wrong, what will I do, how will I cope?"

Or the one that insists, "Whatever happens, I'll handle it"?

Today, go back to the fears list you wrote two weeks ago: all the things that are scaring you. Then, for each item on your list ask yourself, "If this happened, could I handle it?"

Write down the worst that could happen, and how you could respond if it did.

Somehow, you would handle it, wouldn't you... just as you've handled everything else.

Saturday
Expand
There's something about having to read what's being said as well as watch what's happening on screen that involves and immerses you even more completely in the film experience. Today, rent a DVD with subtitles.

Sunday
Explore
Head to the garden center today. There's no need to spend anything. Just allow yourself the pleasure of breathing in the smell of new growth and marveling at the colors and shapes that nature dresses itself in.

Whether you have 100 acres, or a single window box, gather in ideas for how you could bring more color, scent and texture to your little corner of heaven.

Week 18

date....................

Monday
Grow

A healthy, fulfilling life includes healthy relationships. Yet other than watching how other people 'do' relationships, and absorbing beliefs about how they 'should' be from books and films, we're taught very little about how to create healthy relationships in our lives.

A helpful place to start is by understanding that the relationships we have with family members, partners, colleagues and friends are mirrors. The way we relate to people, the way we feel about them and behave when we are with them is always a reflection of who we are, what we believe about ourselves and what we believe about relationships.

There's a wonderful story that illustrates this perfectly.

A traveler arrived at a ferry that would carry him across the river to a new town.

As the ferryman pushed off into the river's current the traveler asked him: "Tell me, what are the people like on the other side of the river?"

The ferryman asked: "What were they like in the last place you lived?"

"Oh," said the traveler. "Mean-spirited, small-minded, rude; mostly they kept themselves to themselves. That's why I'm leaving."

"That's a shame," said the ferryman. "I'm afraid you'll find people much the same on the other side of the river."

The next day he picked up a new passenger who asked the same question.

"What were the people like where you've come from?" the ferryman asked again.

"I'm sorry to be leaving," the passenger replied. *"The people were kind and helpful and looked out for each other. I was very happy there."*

"Let me reassure you," the ferryman replied, *"you'll find them just as warm-hearted where you're going."*

Today and all this week, be on the lookout for the mirror at work. Are you seeing what they are, or what you are?

Tuesday
Receive

Spray or dab a little perfume or eau de toilette on your pillows tonight and enjoy some sweet dreams.

Wednesday
Expand

Most of us find it a lot easier to list what's wrong with us rather than what's right.

But since we've learned that changing our negative sound-track for a more positive one is a key step in changing how we feel, and therefore what we give out and get back, today's activity is another exercise in doing just that.

Grab your journal and, ignoring any blushes and discomfort, write down ten things that you like about your physical appearance, the way you look.

It could be the strength in your arms, your thick hair, the laughter lines around your eyes, the dimple in your elbow.

Be as unconventional as you like, but don't you dare stop until you reach ten, even if you have to count your shapely toes individually (only joking – you may *not*).

Thursday
Give

We all love to be appreciated. Today, write a fan letter to the author of a book that you really enjoyed, or that made a significant difference to your life. You can send it via the publisher, whose address should be on one of the inside pages.

Friday
Connect

The artist Thomas Kinkade reminds us that, "When we keep ourselves tuned to the beauty of the world, life itself becomes a celebration of the senses."

Today, wherever you go and whatever you do, keep yourself tuned to beauty by using all your senses.

Saturday
Commit

This year is all about new experiences, new ideas and new ways of being. But in order to make room for the new, we have to let go of the old. That applies just as much to *things* as it does to thoughts and emotions. Clearing clutter sends a message to our souls that we're in the mood for a shift; it creates space – physically and mentally – and it seems to release energy for other things.

So let's start to clear out the old in order to make way for the new with a spring clean of your car.

How much rubbish are you lugging around? What's lurking in the trunk? And when was the last time you gave your hardworking vehicle a bit of tender loving care in the shape of a wash and polish?

If you don't have a vehicle to lavish TLC on you could give your bike a wash and brush up, or even clear out the shoe cupboard.

Now doesn't that feel good?

Sunday
Explore

Apparently we're slightly taller when we rise each morning than when we went to bed. That's because when we rest our backs the discs that make up the spine get a chance to return to their relaxed state.

Today, take a few minutes out in the middle of the day to give your back a break. Find a flat surface on which to lie on your back. If possible, use a small cushion or even a jumper under your head or neck to align your whole body as straight as you can.

Now bend your knees up, keeping them about shoulder width apart, with your feet still flat on the floor. You should be able to feel your spine coming closer to the floor, supported by it.

Enjoy the sensation of being supported, and notice, when you rise again, whether you feel a fraction taller.

Week 19

date....................

Monday
Receive

Buy a favorite sweet you loved as a child, and eat it without guilt.

Tuesday
Explore

"What is this life if full of care
We have no time to stop and stare?" W.H. Davies

I bet you were taught not to stare, but sometimes it's the only way to see.

Today, make time to stop and stare as often as you possibly can. Look hard at this incredible world.

Wednesday
Commit

When was the last time you peered in the bottom of your handbag or wallet?

We're still on our clear-out kick, in order to make way for new things in our lives.

So take a few minutes to empty the contents of your bag onto the table and be ruthless about throwing out every last sweet wrapper, dog-eared business card and redundant shopping list that really don't need to be there.

Thursday
Grow

Another way of seeing how our relationships mirror us – our thoughts, beliefs and expectations – is to do this exercise:

- Jot down the names of three people you like and the qualities that attract you to them.
- Next do the same for three people you struggle with: people whose behavior rubs you up the wrong way. Alongside their names note what qualities in them make the relationship so difficult.

Now take a good, hard look at what you've written. To what extent does the list reflect you?

To what extent are you drawn to people with qualities you'd like for yourself?

To what extent are the qualities you struggle with in others qualities you dislike in yourself?

If you have a friend who always lets you down, in what ways do you let others – or yourself – down? Or do you have a belief about expecting to be let down?

Are there people in your life who criticize you? If you look in the mirror do you see someone there too who criticizes others, or who is self-critical?

If someone in your life is controlling, are you struggling with that because you like to be in control? Or is it that you believe you should be controlled?

What about your children? Next time you are upset about a child's behavior ask yourself who they are reflecting? Who did they learn that behavior from?

Friday
Expand

This morning when you wake do things in a different order.

Have breakfast before you shower. Don't get dressed until just before you leave. Clean your face before you clean your teeth.

Ringing the changes, even in such tiny ways, jolts us out of our lifelong habit of starting the day on automatic.

Saturday
Give
Today, make a point of noticing all the people whose job it is to help our lives run more smoothly: the postman, the refuse collectors, shop assistants, the folks fixing the road, replacing a streetlight bulb or picking up litter. Choose one of them to thank for doing such a great job.

Or thank them all, if you dare.

Sunday
Connect
"Sooner or later we must realize there is no station, no one place to arrive at once and for all. The true joy of life is the trip." Robert Hastings

So many thinkers and teachers have sought to remind us that it's the journey that matters. Today, don't worry about the destination. Remind yourself often to enjoy the journey.

Week 20

date....................

Monday
Commit

Every culture has had its own way of expressing the fundamental truth: that our thoughts create our world. To change our lives we need to swap thoughts and beliefs that no longer serve us for those that nourish us, as this Native American story puts it so eloquently:

An old Cherokee chief was teaching his grandson about life. "A fight is going on inside me," he said to the boy. "It is a terrible fight between two wolves.

"One is evil – he is anger, envy, sorrow, regret, greed, arrogance, self-pity, guilt, resentment, inferiority, lies, false pride, superiority, self-doubt, and ego.

"The other is good – he is joy, peace, love, hope, serenity, humility, kindness, benevolence, empathy, generosity, truth, compassion, and faith."

He turned to his grandson and said, "This same fight is going on inside you– and inside every other person, too."

The grandson thought about it for a minute and then asked his grandfather, "Which wolf will win?"

The old chief replied simply, "The one you feed."

Which wolf will you choose to feed today?

Tuesday
Receive

Hopefully you're already learning to love and appreciate yourself a little more, one day at a time. Today's activity gives you a chance to build on that by drawing on your own life story to finish these statements in your journal:

- It was generous of me to...
- I was kind when I...
- I was a really good friend when...
- I did a good job when...
- I went the extra mile when ...
- I deserve a medal for...

See how much there is to appreciate about you?

Wednesday
Explore

Today, look up at the sky every single chance you get. Watch it change shape and shade. Observe its moods. Notice how it is ever shifting.

And each time you look up remember the billions of others living their lives under the same, endless sky. I find that as I look up from my small, everyday concerns into its vastness some of the things that bother me shrink in size, and seem less important than I've built them up to be.

Thursday
Connect

"There are only two ways to live your life. One is as though nothing is a miracle. The other is as though everything is a miracle." Albert Einstein

Today believe in miracles, expect miracles, and be on the lookout for miracles.

Friday
Give

Raise a late night smile by putting a chocolate on everyone's pillow tonight and turning down the covers (after all, you've almost certainly been heard to complain that people treat the place like a hotel).

Saturday
Expand

Throughout history people have understood the connection between the mind and body. Vibrant health begins in the mind and when we're struggling in some part of our lives it often reveals itself as sickness or ill health.

The most obvious place to see this at work is with accidents. Often it's because we're stressed, preoccupied, careless (caring-less about ourselves) that we experience an accident.

Or, when you're soldiering on, overwhelmed by the demands on your time and energy, insisting you're too busy to take even a moment off, then wham, you succumb to a cold or flu that forces you to take the break you need.

Today, begin to expand your understanding of the relationship between mind and body by getting hold of Louise Hay's groundbreaking *Heal Your Body* book, which offers a way of understanding certain ailments, aches and pains as they may relate to what's going on in the rest of our lives. (You'll also find this guide in the back of *You Can Heal Your Life®*.)

Sunday
Grow

If relationships are mirrors, does the face we present truly belong to us, or are we actually reflecting thoughts and beliefs we learned from others?

Today, spend a short time trying to understand any beliefs you may have about how relationships 'should' be that no longer serve you. Like everything else in our lives, we learned how to do them, what to believe about them, and what to expect from them from the people we were around while we were growing up.

In your journal, write down the words that come to mind when you think about your parents' or carer's relationships with you, with each other, and with their wider networks. In particular, what were their strengths and weaknesses?

Now go through those lists and put a tick against each of those which could also apply to you in *your* relationships.

Ask yourself whether the relationships you've based your own beliefs on were good examples. If not, are you ready to change? We don't have to live what we learned. We can make different choices. What kind of example would you want your own relationships to set for others?

Week 21

date....................

Monday
Expand
We're bombarded with bad news on all sides. Give yourself a break this week and give up on newspapers and the TV news. Rest assured, if anything major happens, someone will tell you. Meanwhile, you get a week's respite from a non-stop diet of negative messages that's just guaranteed to bring you down.

Tuesday
Receive
"The most wasted day is that in which we have not laughed." Nicolas de Chamfort

Today, rent a movie that makes you laugh aloud, or find an old sitcom on one of the TV channels. Award yourself the time to sit and enjoy it, and to laugh loud and long without worrying you'll sound silly.

Wednesday
Connect
"If you don't like something, change it.

If you can't change it, change your attitude." Maya Angelou

Today, remember you're in control of how you think your life and therefore how you live your life.

Thursday
Explore
Staying with last week's theme of the relationship between our minds and our health, our bodies are wonderful feedback devices when it comes to telling us what's going on in our lives.

So what's yours telling you at the moment?

One way to get in touch with your body's voice is through meditation. Using any of the meditation techniques you've learned, get your body into a peaceful state and become aware of any place in your body where there is soreness, pain or stiffness.

Gently place your hand onto that place and ask your body to tell you what is wrong.

Then simply wait quietly for your body's inner wisdom to tell you what is causing the discomfort.

Before you leave your meditation, imagine your hand is a healer's hand, and your touch is bringing warmth, light and healing into the part of your body where it is resting.

Is there something you need to do or change or think about as a result of hearing your body's message?

Friday
Grow
So what do you need from your relationships?

A healthy relationship is one in which we're able to be the best we can be; its opposite is one that somehow diminishes us.

As a starting point, write a list of the things you want from your relationships. To help you, you might like to think back to those relationships that have really worked – with friends, family, partners, colleagues.

What do you need: respect, entertainment, fun, protection, stimulation, learning, nurture, equality, unconditional love? Write it all down.

One sign we're growing up is when we realize that outside the pages of fiction we're unlikely to get all our needs met in a single relationship. (And wouldn't life be boring if one was all we needed?)

So now you've got your list of needs, try matching it up to the significant relationships in your life right now. Are you getting enough of your needs met enough of the time?

And if not, where *are* you going to get these things from? Do you need to make new friends, meet new partners, or put more work into your existing relationships?

As you work at this, remind yourself that we get what we give. If relationships are mirrors, then the most effective way to change the relationship is to change ourselves.

Go through all the items on your 'needs-list' again and ask yourself honestly, "Do I give this to the people in my life?" For example, if you want to be loved for who you are, to what extent do you love others unconditionally?

Saturday
Commit

Some people seem to have no trouble standing up for themselves, but assertiveness is not the same as bad manners or rudeness. It's about valuing yourself and your opinions as much as you value those of others. And learning and practicing good communications skills in order to express your thoughts, feelings and beliefs in a straightforward, honest and appropriate way.

Today's exercise is a crash course in assertiveness to help you fill a you-sized space in the world, rather than shrinking from your own shadow. Choose one or two points from the list below to try out today.

- *Use 'I' messages*: "I find it hard to plan my day because I never know what time you're coming" is more effective than "You're always late" which is a criticism. Talking about the effect of their behavior on you is less threatening.
- *Use facts rather than judgments*: "I have been waiting for you to do the housework as we agreed" is better than sweeping statements such as "You're so lazy". And keep to one fact to make your point: rehashing 10 years' worth of wrangles is likely to be counter-productive.
- *Own your feelings*: "*I'm angry* that you made this decision without me" rather than "*You've made me* angry". You don't

have to apologize for how you feel: your feelings are your early warning system telling you something is amiss in your world – and you're the expert on them.

- *Use direct words*: 'no' rather than 'I don't think so'; 'yes' rather than 'if you like'. Trying to sweeten the message is a very easy trap to fall into, but remember we're all very good at hearing what we want to hear so the clearer you are the less scope there is for misunderstandings.

- *Make sure your expression matches your message*: and maintain eye contact. Sometimes when we're feeling awkward we smile or look away, even though we're very serious about the words we're speaking. So much of what we communicate is done through our body language, your mixed messages are bound to confuse.

- *Write down the key points you want to make and practice them* in advance so you can stay focused. It may sound a bit staged, and as you get better at speaking up for yourself you may no longer need to do it. But knowing what you want to say is especially helpful when you're dealing with a verbal conjuror. If they start down that track you can simply repeat the points you've practiced over again, refusing to get into an argument.

- *Listen carefully to any response* and let them know you've heard – but remember, there's a difference between listening and having to win the argument. You're fully entitled to express yourself; they don't have to agree with you.

Sunday
Give
Today, give someone a short hand massage. It's a treat often used by therapists in hospitals and residential homes precisely because having someone stroke our hands is so soothing and nurturing. Holding someone's hand has always been a way of

communicating our love and support for them.

Get your silkiest hand cream, find your volunteer and invite them to close their eyes and enjoy a few minutes of pampering. Who knows, they may even offer you one back.

Week 22

date....................

Monday
Commit

Practice mindfulness again today. Instead of paying attention to *your* life, pay attention to those you meet, down to the smallest details of how they speak, the words they use, how they move, how they dress, their gestures, habits and what they give out.

Humankind is so wonderfully fascinating and varied.

Tuesday
Give

Put a bag of small change in your car or pocket so you can help out anyone who hasn't got change for the parking meter.

Wednesday
Expand

Last week we looked at being more assertive. Today, continue to practice what you learned by saying "yes" when you mean "yes" and "no" when you mean "no". No justifying yourself, or qualifying what you want with explanations, excuses and apologies.

See how it feels to express your feelings directly in this way and be aware of any reaction your honesty provokes – in yourself as well as in those on the receiving end.

Thursday
Grow

A really useful tool for shifting our most challenging relationships is to make a conscious effort to see the world through others' eyes, or, as the Native Americans say, "To walk a mile in their moccasins."

Whenever people seem to you to be behaving badly or being deliberately difficult, moving out of your own thoughts, reactions and emotions and into theirs will have a profound effect on the way you respond to them.

Try this technique out now by thinking back to a recent argument or issue between you and someone in your life.

Close your eyes and imagine yourself in their body looking at you and hearing the things you are saying. What's going on in their head? What are they feeling? What emotions are they experiencing? *What lies behind the words and the feelings?*

Now when you move back into your own body use your new understanding of them to consider is there anything you'd do or say differently?

Friday
Receive
Find a large bottle, empty container, or piggy bank, and label it 'dream fund'. Every time you have loose change in your pocket or purse, empty it into your fund. It's amazing how little amounts add up, especially once you start to fantasize about which of your dreams you intend to make come true, using your savings. You could even stick a picture on it, to spur you on to dig a little deeper.

Just a reminder, even if you take only small steps, eventually you'll get wherever you aim to be. Your dreams *are* on their way.

Saturday
Explore
Today, find somewhere to experience the feel of wind on your face. We talk about it being a windy day as if wind was a nuisance rather than a reminder of how the wind of change can be such a positive energy.

Close your eyes. Ponder on how far the wind has traveled to reach you. And really experience its touch on your skin and your hair. Imagine breathing in the wind so it can spring clean the cobwebs from your soul.

Sunday
Connect

Something for you to think about today:

How would your life be different if you really knew that you are always doing the best you can?

Why would anyone expect more than that? Why would you?

Week 23

date.....................

Monday
Connect

"Nothing can bring you peace but yourself." Ralph Waldo Emerson

Today, do everything peacefully. Let go of any thoughts that disturb or agitate you, express the peace you are seeking in your relationships, in your work, in your home, and in your heart.

Be at peace.

Tuesday
Commit

There are so many ways in which choosing to focus on positive rather than negative thoughts changes the way we experience the world.

Today, make a list of people you dislike or have real difficulty with. Then find *at least* two positive things to say about each of them. OK, so they may be opinionated: that means they speak their mind and you know where you are with them.

Perhaps they're lazy... and could therefore teach *you* a thing or two about slowing down and not sweating the small stuff.

Wednesday
Give

Encourage wildlife into your garden or backyard by leaving out treats. For instance, hedgehogs love milk and will be only too happy to do you a favor in return by gobbling up slugs.

If you don't have a garden, then plant something colorful to attract butterflies or hang a bird feeder. Having lots of life around is good for the soul.

Thursday
Expand
Wear some really 'loud' jewelry today. Surprise people and surprise yourself, by drawing attention to you.

Friday
Receive
When I was small my favorite ice cream was a rocket-shaped orange and strawberry ice pop, topped with vanilla and covered in chocolate.

Today, treat yourself to a good rummage in the ice cream cabinet, bypassing all those sensible grown-up tastes to select a child's ice cream with as many colors and gimmicks and flavors as you can find. Fun on a stick!

Saturday
Grow
Sometimes life seems to be just one long list of 'must do's'. So much so that it's easy to forget we always have a choice.

From now on, whenever you catch yourself using the words **'should'**, **'have to'** and **'must'** try replacing them with '**could**' – a simple technique to remind you that you're the one making the choices.

- Try it out now by jotting down a few of your 'shoulds': what should you do or be?
- Next, for each item on your list ask yourself, "Why should I?" Write down your answers, and pay close attention to where the 'should' is coming from: whose thought or belief is behind it? Who said you should?
- Finally, replace each 'should' with 'could', and notice whether it changes the way you feel.

Sunday
Explore
Go foraging in nature to find something for your larder. Fruit, nuts, leaves, even 'weeds': there's an abundance of free foods out there and books to consult if you lack the confidence to track down wild garlic, or nettles for a vitamin-packed soup by yourself.

Week 24

date...................

Monday
Grow

Remember me saying that we teach people how to treat us by how we treat ourselves?

Your task as you go through this day is to observe your own behavior and pay close attention to the messages you're giving out to others about how to treat you.

For example, are you pushing yourself too hard, overcommitting, letting people know they can push you too? There's a reason for the saying that if you want something done you should ask a busy person!

Are you treating yourself with respect? Or putting yourself down, letting people know they can put you down?

Are you taking care of your own needs or teaching others you don't mind being at the back of every line?

Be honest. And as you identify what you're teaching, consider whether it's time for a new lesson plan.

Tuesday
Explore

Get a book or DVD from the library on yoga and teach yourself a yoga pose. You could choose a simple position that you can use to calm and center yourself when you're feeling stressed, or perhaps one that gives you that wonderful sense of really inhabiting your body by gently stretching and expanding it. Alternatively, teach yourself a pose to adopt during meditation.

Wednesday
Expand

Today, try a herbal tea, or a new flavor if you're already a fan. There are some fantastic combinations on the shelves now and unlike caffeine-laden tea and coffee, herbal drinks are kind to your system.

Thursday
Commit

When you feel the need to relax but haven't time for a walk a useful technique to use is to go on a mental holiday. Believe it or not, our bodies find it hard to distinguish between real events and those we recreate in our minds, which is why just thinking about a favorite food can make your mouth water, and why your heart races when you're watching a scary TV drama. Recreating a memory of being relaxed in your mind will slow your heart rate and settle your mind almost as if it were really happening.

So close your eyes and remember a time when you felt happy, relaxed and at peace. Perhaps you were sitting at the seashore gazing out over the endless blue. Or in the hills, breathing pure oxygen. Or with a loved one, laughing, sharing a special moment.

Once you've identified your memory then picture all the details in your mind as thoroughly as you can: what you could see, smell, taste, hear, touch, but above all how you felt. Allow your breathing to settle down as you recall the peace, beauty and joy of that time. If you like, you may also want to use the affirmation "I am relaxed and at peace in my mind and in my life".

Store that memory to return to whenever you need a moment's breathing space.

Friday
Connect

Something to think about:

"A man is just about as happy as he makes up his mind to be."
Abraham Lincoln

Now you understand how your thoughts create your experience, how happy will you choose to be today?

Saturday
Receive

Treat yourself to a color consultation: we might feel comfortably anonymous in brown and black but learning to appreciate ourselves means knowing which colors really complement our skin tones and bring us alive.

If you can't stretch to a professional consultation then get together with a few friends and *lots* of scarves. Take turns wrapping the various shades around your necks in front of a large mirror. You can advise each other on which colors enhance the way you look and which drain the color from you.

Sunday
Give

Take flowers to a graveyard and spread them between a few of the headstones that look neglected. Just because people are anonymous in death doesn't mean they didn't make a contribution in life.

Week 25

date....................

Monday
Commit

Back to clearing clutter in order to make way for the new: how often do you decide not to start on something that needs doing simply because the task seems so huge?

The truth is, we can manage almost anything if we tackle it a bit at a time – rather like this book. Today, choose a drawer – just one – to overhaul. It could be in your kitchen, bathroom, dining room or cellar. Turn it out, give it a good clean, and only put back the things you *know* you're going to use.

In the interests of avoiding overwhelm, resist the temptation to carry on and do the rest now you've started.

Tuesday
Connect

Something to think about:

"We don't see things as they are. We see things as we are." Anaïs Nin

Today, open your eyes to the possibility that everything is not as it seems to you.

Wednesday
Give

Scan the newspapers or listen out for someone having a hard time at the moment. Send them a short message of sympathy and support. Sometimes the effects of a gesture like this are even more powerful because the message is coming from a stranger.

Thursday
Grow

In the end it keeps coming back to what we choose to think and believe. So today, let's look at what you believe about wealth and abundance.

Hard to come by? Never enough? It's not nice to want more? What we give out is what we get back, so becoming aware of your thoughts is the first stage in deciding whether it's time to choose new ones.

In your journal, write down the thoughts that come to mind when money or wealth are mentioned. What did you learn when you were growing up from your parents and teachers? What were your early experiences around money like? (A clue to help you here – if you want to know what you believe, take a good look at your relationship with money now.)

Are these beliefs serving you well? Or does it bring you down to have them playing in your head?

Is it time to tune into some new thoughts around abundance?

Friday
Receive
Buy some Rescue® Remedy from a health or drug store, to carry in your bag for moments of high emotion when you really need to take care of yourself.

Saturday
Explore
Make friends with a tree today: choose a tree to befriend and, once you have, put your arms as far around it as you can and feel how solid it is. Put your ear to the bark and see if you can hear the tree's heartbeat. Look up into the canopy and notice how something so strong is also so flexible. Imagine all the things your tree has seen and lived through.

Make a note of where your new friend is so you can revisit from time to time and get to know it through the seasons.

Sunday
Expand
Poetry is written to be heard so become a poetry reader today. You could choose a poem with wonderful rhymes that you enjoyed as a child. Or pick up that anthology that's gathering dust on the shelf and see what you happen on.

Among my favorites to recite aloud are the poems of Mary Oliver, rich with wonderful observations and language.

Ignore any awkwardness about the sound of your voice. This will almost certainly be a hangover from schooldays and being forced to stand up and read aloud in class. Today your performance is for your ears only.

Week 26

date...................

Monday
Expand

When we get stuck, so does the dial on the radio. Choose a different station to listen to today. If your dial's stuck on music, listen to a documentary or a play. If you're hooked on angry phone-ins, retune to a classical station and experience some peace.

Tuesday
Grow

In order to bring more abundance into our lives we need to develop an abundance consciousness. You can see this at work in the world all the time. There are people with the Midas touch, who just can't seem to help turning every venture into gold. Conversely, we read about lottery winners losing it all because they just don't see themselves as rich.

One way of starting to shift our personal abundance consciousness is to understand that we really are in control. While we're busy believing money – or lack of money – is controlling our lives, every day we're actually making dozens of choices about where wealth fits into our priorities.

See it for yourself with this exercise:

- In your journal write down at least five ways in which you could spend less money, for instance making a packed lunch instead of buying sandwiches, turning the heating down, staying in more instead of going out. *You don't have to like them* and you certainly don't have to do them; just humor me by writing them all down.
- Next, write down at least five ways in which you could earn more money, for instance taking in a lodger, getting a

second part-time job, or selling stuff on eBay. Again, remember the point is just to identify what you *could* do if you really wanted to. You don't have to do any of this.

Now do you see that, once again, you have a choice? If having more money in your bank account was your number one priority you could choose to do those things.

Most of us prefer to strike a balance, recognizing that having time to ourselves, being warm, seeing our friends, buying a gift for a loved one make us happier than squirreling away every spare penny.

We're more in control than we thought, and knowing that is a positive step in the direction of altering our sometimes troublesome relationship with money and wealth. If you want to go a step further, there are many excellent books that can also help you take *more* control by becoming an active manager of your money, among my favorites Michael Neill's chapter on money in his book *You Can Have What You Want*.

Wednesday
Connect
"The gift turned inward, unable to be given, becomes a heavy burden, even sometimes a kind of poison. It is as though the flow of life were backed up." May Sarton

What are your unique gifts? Would you have been given them if you weren't intended to use them?

To what extent *do* you use your gifts in the life you've created? Or are they backed up, blocking the flow of life?

Thursday
Receive
No matter how much love we may have in our lives, many of us go short on the comfort of human touch.

Tonight, grab a bottle of your favorite body lotion and spend five minutes massaging it into your skin, stroking your own body, from the nape of your neck down to your toes. Take your time. Enjoy not only being touched, but the touching too.

Friday
Explore
Eat a meal outdoors today and notice how much more flavorsome it is.

Saturday
Commit
Another way in which we can practice mindfulness is by slowing down.

Rushing and busy-ness are modern addictions which keep us from enjoying the moment we're in. It's amazing what a difference even small shifts can make to our awareness and sense of well-being, such as walking to the shops instead of jumping in the car. Or taking the time to cook a meal from scratch rather than bunging something in the microwave.

Whenever you can today *choose the slower option*. Do everything at a comfortable rather than a frantic pace, and give yourself permission not to worry about getting absolutely everything done.

Chances are, it will. You do remember the fable of the hare and the tortoise don't you?

Sunday
Give
Buy a packet of wildflower seeds and scatter them in a public place or alongside the road to surprise and delight passers-by a few months from now.

Week 27

date....................

Monday
Explore

Today, discover what it really means to be a human *being*. Find a lovely spot to sit outdoors and just 'be' for no less than 20 minutes – the longer the better.

Do *nothing* except watch, listen, smell, notice and enjoy.

You'll almost certainly find yourself getting restless and wanting to get up and get busy. But, just this once, sit through it. Peace takes practice. If it helps you to stay put tell yourself you're under orders from me.

I promise, if you give peace a chance, there'll come a moment when it settles softly on your shoulders and into your soul.

Tuesday
Expand

Spend some time today talking to someone you don't know well. Find out about their lives and their views. Make an effort to get to know them a little.

Who knows what you might be setting in train?

Wednesday
Commit

Get in the habit of having something more positive than phone-ins to listen to on the journey to work. Most of the authors I've listed at the back of this book are also available on CD as audio-books, or you can download talking books or podcasts of their work onto your MP3.

If you need help deciding where to start, the CD I wouldn't be without is Wayne Dyer and Byron Katie's *Making Your Thoughts Work For You*: four discs packed so full of wisdom that every time I listen I hear something new.

You'll know you're on the right track when you find yourself hoping the traffic jam goes on just a little longer so you can finish listening.

Thursday
Give
Animal sanctuaries depend on donations of time and goods. Support their work by taking a few cans of pet food to an animal shelter, or leave them in the collection box at your nearest pet superstore.

Friday
Grow
Another way of tuning into a consciousness of abundance rather than lack is to practice gratitude. There are so many ways in which, if we expand our understanding of what wealth is, we realize we're already rich beyond measure.

Hopefully, gratitude is now part of your daily practice, but this exercise is another way of seeing even more clearly how abundance is flowing in your life:

- In your journal list as many of the ways in which you've received abundance in the last month as you can recall. It could be anything from an unexpected gift, a friend buying you lunch, to a beautiful day on which you felt truly blessed.
- Next list some of the ways in which *you've* shared abundance with others. Perhaps you dropped a few coins into a charity box, donated your time to a good cause, passed on a favorite book or took the kids for a day out.

As we broaden our understanding of what abundance looks like we notice it starting to show up in many shapes and forms. Coins and notes are only one small way in which we exchange it and allow its flow throughout our lives.

Saturday
Receive
Become a traveler today, without leaving home. Visit America by cooking pancakes with syrup, watching reruns of your favorite US TV series and wearing your Levis.

Or, if you're already in America, go European. Have croissants and hot chocolate for breakfast, watch a Spanish soccer game and wear a beret.

Sunday
Connect
"May you live all the days of your life." Jonathan Swift

What would it take for you to be truly alive in this day? To properly live it?

Week 28

date....................

Monday
Connect

Something to think about today and every day:

"If you have a choice to be right or to be kind, be kind." Anon

Notice when it seems to matter to you to be right. Ask yourself why it matters so much. Could you let that go? See what difference it makes when you choose being kind over being right.

Tuesday
Grow

What do you believe about work? Do you live to work or work to live?

Is work always *hard*: hard at work, work hard, hard-working? Are your beliefs about work getting in the way of you finding fulfilling and rewarding work? Or are you already doing the work you were born to do?

One way of drilling down to discover our beliefs about work is to look at what you liked and disliked about each job you've done. You can include volunteering and other unpaid work, including work in the home, if you like.

- Thinking about each of the jobs you've had, write down in your journal two or three statements that express how you felt about that role. For example, "I was able to use my talents", "I felt valued and appreciated"; or "my colleagues drove me crazy", "my job was too stressful", "I was underpaid for what I did".
- Now go through all those statements and see if any come up more than once.
- Wherever you find a pattern you're unearthing a belief you need to be aware of, in case it's holding you back.

Wednesday
Receive

Tonight, turn bath time into a blissful sanctuary. Fetch as many candles as you can to light the corners of the room, select your sweetest-smelling oil or bubbles and a glass of cold wine or fruit juice. Hang a 'do not disturb' sign on the door and relax into another of life's simple pleasures.

You'd take the time to have a bath anyway. How often do you take the same time and turn it into a treat?

Thursday
Give

Be kind to animals and to the planet. Go vegetarian for the day (or the week if you're feeling adventurous).

Friday
Expand

Get some crayons and make an inspirational poster to stick up inside your wardrobe door to serve as a big, bright, colorful reminder to you every day of your life.

How about: 'Today is the best day of my life'....or 'If not now, when?'...or 'Good morning, beautiful!'

Saturday
Commit

Creative visualization is a popular technique for 'manifesting' in our lives the changes we want to bring about. Like affirmations, visualization works by changing our feelings, and therefore the energy we give out. "The way you think is the way you feel and the way you feel is the way you vibrate and the way you vibrate is the way you attract", as Lynn Grabhorn puts it so succinctly in a book that will really inspire you, *Excuse Me, Your Life is Waiting*.

- Have a go now by closing your eyes and picturing

something you want wrapped up in a huge gift box. It doesn't matter if it's not a 'thing': if you've chosen a happy loving relationship or a promotion at work simply picture the actual event or something that symbolizes it in your gift box.

- Keeping your eyes closed and breathing peacefully, imagine yourself going to the front door and finding the parcel there. It has a big label with your name on it. Look at the wrapping paper and the glittering ribbon. Picture yourself peeling off the layers of paper and tissue, peering into the box and your excitement at discovering your dream right there in front of you.
- Take a few moments to just feel your pleasure and excitement before gently opening your eyes.

Since it's all about changing how you feel, you can also use visualization if you're facing a challenging situation or want something to go well. Close your eyes and picture the situation as clearly as you can, imagine it all working out for the best.

A great resource if you want to explore this tool more fully is Shakti Gawain's *Creative Visualization*.

Sunday
Explore
Can you remember what fun it was to wade when you were young? Today, roll up your trouser legs and find a pool to cool your toes in. Or head for the riverbank and dangle your feet into the water.

Some sensations are as wonderful whether we're six or 60.

Week 29

date...................

Monday
Grow

According to Katherine Whitehaven, "The best career advice to give the young is find out what you like doing best and get someone to pay you for doing it."

What do you love doing? When are you at your happiest, most involved and fulfilled?

Perhaps you're already doing it, in which case ask yourself if there's anything that would make it even more fulfilling?

If you're not sure, a useful question to ask yourself is would you continue to do the job you're doing even if you weren't being paid to do it?

Unless you can answer yes then you've still to find the perfect work for you.

So make a start today by heeding Whitehaven's advice and brainstorming in your journal all the ways in which you could turn your passion – the things you like doing best – into work you can make money from.

Even if you don't believe it's practical right now, allow yourself to play with the possibilities. Remember, none of us knows how huge the seed of an idea may grow.

Tuesday
Connect

Something to think about:

"Time is the coin of your life. It is the only coin you have, and only you can determine how it will be spent. Be careful lest you let other people spend it for you." Carl Sandburg

How much of every 24 hours do you decide how to spend those coins? And how much of the time do others have control of your purse?

Wednesday
Commit

Apart from helping us shift into a more positive frame of mind, visualization is a wonderful tool for solving problems and getting in touch with our own inner wisdom.

There are many guided visualizations to try, designed to lead your subconscious through a particular issue that's troubling you and to the wise voice that lies at the heart of all of us.

Some of the books in the recommended reading list, particularly Gill Edwards' books, are packed with suggestions for guided visualizations you can use to address specific issues and questions in your life.

But you may find it easier, particularly at the start, to use a tape or CD in which someone talks you through the process. Search 'guided visualizations' on the Internet or see what you can find on the shelves of the local library or bookstore.

Thursday
Receive

In your journal write a list of all the things your soul really loves. The list could include music that stirs you, a taste you adore, your favorite smells, or the views that melt your heart. It could include people, places, things....whatever it is that makes your life worth living.

I hope your list is a really long one, and that before you've finished writing it you've decided to treat yourself to at least one thing on your love list today.

Friday
Expand

Learn a little about essential oils and how to use them for health and well-being. There are plenty of books in the library and lots of information online. I always use a few drops of lavender in the bath if there are cuts and scrapes that need healing; clary sage when I'm feeling a little low; and eucalyptus on the pillow for colds and snuffles.

Saturday
Explore
Take your camera or camera-phone on an artistic journey today. Choose an ordinary street near your home, or a part of the town center that you think you know well.

Now see the scene as an artist might, allowing yourself to notice details you've never spotted before, the way different elements relate to and contrast with each other, as you search for interesting shots to capture.

Sunday
Give
A few weeks ago you read some poetry aloud. Today, give the gift of poetry to others. Copy or write out one of your favorites, cover it in plastic and stick it up at a bus shelter or anywhere else that people have to wait.

Who knows what a difference your small act of kindness may make to someone's day?

Week 30

date....................

Monday
Connect

"Do you think you can take over the universe and improve it?"
from The Tao

Whatever you are doing today, let go of the controls a little. For so much of our lives we give ourselves a hard time by trying to control other people and events.

Today, let the Universe handle it for you.

Tuesday
Receive

Today, buy a pack of ice popsicles and freeze them. The next time it's a hot day fetch your favorite flavor from the freezer and remember how wonderful it was to be a child on a hot day when the ice pops came out.(Don't forget to stick your tongue out at the mirror before you're done and see what color it's turned!)

Wednesday
Expand

We may joke that 'it's a sign' but looking out for and reading signs has been an important part of seeking guidance in many cultures throughout history.

Indeed, once we open our minds to the messages that are all around us, we see we are surrounded by signs: the soaring eagle telling us to take flight; the song that's speaking directly to us when we turn on the radio; the heart-shaped stone washed up on the beach reminding us that we'll heal.

During a period when I struggling with a major decision that would turn my life on its head I rented a cottage in the hills to do some thinking. As I unlocked the front door my eyes were caught by a picture on the opposite wall with the title 'Laying a foundation stone'. I switched on the TV and *Groundhog Day* was showing, a clear sign that nothing would change unless I did. Then, at dusk I went for a walk and came across a field of dragon-flies, reassuring me I was going through a major transformation and to enjoy the process.

Today, identify an area in your life where you are lost, confused, or in need of guidance. Quietly ask for a sign. Then, throughout the day, keep your eyes open and your ears attuned for it to show up.

Thursday
Explore
Put a pair of binoculars by a window so you can watch the birds in the street, the garden or on next door's roof. They'll also be handy for looking at the stars on a clear night.

If you don't own a pair, yard sales are a good source for cheap second-hand binoculars.

Friday
Grow
Here's another exercise that may help you identify ways in which you can change your working life, or change your attitude to it.

Before you write anything, close your eyes for a few moments, focus on breathing deeply, drop your shoulders, relax the muscles in your face, and feel your feet solid on the ground.

Then, when you are ready, ask yourself:

- If I had the power to change anything about my current working situation what would it be?
- What would my ideal colleagues be like and how would they behave?
- What are six words that describe my ideal working situation?
- Finally, if tomorrow I heard that I had won, say, $200,000 or

£100,000 – enough to buy some thinking time, or to start a business, to leave my current job and take time out to think about what I'd like to do – then what work would I create? The only condition is that this money must be spent on my working life.

Your answers will help you identify not only what you might want to change but areas where you might want to change your attitude.

Saturday
Give
Pass onto one of your friends an article or book that touched, helped or inspired you.

Sunday
Commit
Picking up the threads of the life story you've been recording, write about a time when you were disappointed and any consequences that followed on.

Week 31

date....................

Monday
Receive

Curl up on the sofa with a cuddly toy and watch a children's program on TV today.

Tuesday
Explore

A useful technique for taking care of ourselves is to learn how to scan our bodies for tension. When we're stressed we tend to tighten everything, which just makes it harder for our energy to flow.

Close your eyes and working from your head down, become aware of any places that are tight or sore. Are the muscles on your forehead or around your mouth clenched? Are your shoulders hunched? Are you gripping fresh air with your hands? Are your legs tight, poised to dash onto the next thing?

As you move through your body, consciously loosen and slacken all those tight places. Drop your shoulders, imagine the lines on your face smoothing out, imagine yourself breathing relaxation into your muscles and your body as loose and fluid as water.

Remember to do this any time in the future when tension, stress or difficult emotions have got your body in a vice-like grip.

Wednesday
Commit

Isn't it amazing how almost everything looks at least a little better after a decent night's sleep? How hearing someone else's bad news can suddenly make some of our worries seem trivial? How as we grow older we find ourselves smiling at the memory of the things that used to make us anxious?

It's all down to perspective, but we don't have to wait for bad news or to grow older to inject a little more of it into our lives.

Today, jot down a few of the things that are troubling or annoying you, from major concerns to minor niggles.

Now work through them, one at a time, asking yourself: will this still worry me a week from now? Will it still worry me a year from now? Will it still worry me in 10 years' time?

If you're going to let it go soon, sometime or eventually, then why not now?

Thursday
Expand

How good are you at asking for help? For some reason most of us seem to find it easier to give than to receive, to respond to a request for help rather than to make our own.

Now you've had some practice at speaking up for yourself, let's extend the comfort zone a fraction more by doing just that. Today, ask someone for help with something.

Friday
Connect

"The real voyage of discovery consists not in seeing new landscapes but in having new eyes." Marcel Proust

In other words, you don't need to travel to experience new things, think new thoughts, see things differently. Today, try out a new set of eyes.

Saturday
Give

Have you heard of craigslist or freecycle? Both are free online services where you can find a new home for something you no longer need. Take a look around your home and see what you're ready to pass on to someone who will love and value it.

If you're not online, most cities now have charity furniture stores that will come and collect items in good condition to pass onto those who need them, raising funds at the same time.

Sunday
Grow

Picture perfect models, extreme makeovers, ads for cosmetic surgery – it doesn't matter where you look, it seems that we're just not good enough the way we are. Is it any wonder that so many of us suffer from fragile self-esteem?

Believe it or not it wasn't always that way. Most of us, if we're lucky, are born with oodles of the stuff. Just watch a baby at the center of the whole universe, with no inhibitions about demanding exactly what it wants when it wants it. How soon we lose that sense of ourselves as perfectly OK depends on the world we encounter, the amount of love and respect we receive and what we absorb from the people around us: parents, carers, family, friends, teachers, then later colleagues and boyfriends/girlfriends.

Plus, of course, the world in which we live; a world that seems, on the face of it at least, to value us by what we *do, earn* or *own,* and by how we *look,* rather than for who we are.

To esteem yourself means treating yourself the way you would anything you value, respect or love, such as a dear friend.

It means treating yourself with care and appreciation. It means not giving yourself a hard time, accepting that even though there are things you may want to change or improve you're doing the best you can. It means focusing on the positive rather than the negative and becoming your own best friend.

All themes we're already working on this year, but while you're slowly learning how to love and appreciate yourself a little more it's always useful to have a few instant self-esteem boosters up your sleeve.

An effective way to instantly boost your self-esteem is to focus on what you're good at.

When we're good at something we usually forget to be self-critical, we get recognition for what we do, feel good about being praised, and find it even easier to do well.

So whether you're a whizz at figures, can make cakes light as air, or are a warm and intuitive listener who friends always seek out when they're in trouble, write down in your journal all those things you are good at.

And maybe a couple you're brilliant at...

Before you leave your list think about how you can make more opportunities in your life to do those things.

Week 32

date....................

Monday
Receive

Today, instead of worrying about the To Do list focus on what you've done. At the end of the day write out your Done List: paid the bills, cooked an amazing meal, managed to fit in a phone call to your best friend, and so on. Now give yourself a huge pat on the back. It's awesome what you achieved in just one short day.

Tuesday
Expand

Are you still asking permission to breathe? Living your life on approval – other people's?

In order to live authentic lives we must give up the need for everyone's approval, to be people pleasers at the expense of our own instincts, desires and dreams. We waste so much time explaining and justifying ourselves when the truth is we're unlikely to ever please everyone.

Once upon a time our carers did know what was best for us but we're grown-ups now.

As you go through today, be aware of every time that you are subconsciously seeking approval for the things you say, do and are.

And when you spot them, tell yourself that you approve of you and that's what matters most.

Wednesday
Grow

Another way to smooth talk our self-esteem a notch or two higher is by celebrating our successes.

In your journal, start an audit of all that you've achieved. Few of us get to pick up an Oscar but that doesn't mean our lives aren't full of hundreds of small successes, from learning to load photos onto the Internet to managing the food budget each week.

Start your success list today and don't stop until you've recorded at least 15 of your achievements and successes.

Don't forget, either, that you can continue to add to your list each time you pull off a new recipe, pick the perfect present for your best friend, bite your tongue rather than biting back, or learn to swim butterfly.

Thursday
Connect

"As much as we watch to see what our children do in their lives, they are watching us to see what we do with ours. I can't tell my children to reach for the sun. All I can do is reach for it, myself."
Joyce Maynard

We learn by example, remember? Whether or not you have children, consider what kind of example your life is setting. What are the ways in which *your* life inspires, teaches and motivates others, maybe even to reach for the sun?

Friday
Give

Enter a competition today in someone else's name. Local newspapers and magazines are a good source of easy-to-enter contests.

Saturday
Commit

It's been a while since we did any clearing out so today I want you to tackle the shed, a corner of the garage, or a cupboard. Don't forget, every single time we clear out the unwanted we're making space in our lives and freeing up energy.

If you've enjoyed that feeling of lightness that accompanies each clearing-out session then why not schedule a few more sessions in the coming weeks? Ideas might include your jewelry box, the files on your computer, more cupboards, the attic, or behind the settee.

It's great therapy, especially if you put on some uplifting music while you're decluttering.

Now there's another idea: when did you last weed out your music collection to make way for the new?

Sunday
Explore

Today, give your body a detox. Eat only fruit and veg, and drink only water and juices. Visualize these good foods flushing your system clean and filling you with vibrant health.

Week 33

date....................

Monday
Grow

Last week we looked at boosting self-esteem by celebrating our achievements. But not every success in our lives starts out looking that way.

As the film star Mary Pickford said: "This thing we call failure is not the falling down but the staying down."

Today, note down a few of the times in your life when you've failed, fallen, or been knocked down – and managed to pick yourself up, dust yourself off, and get on with your life.

Believe me, these are your biggest successes.

Tuesday
Connect

"Think before you speak is criticism's motto; speak before you think, creation's." E.M. Forster

How often do you stifle your own authentic voice?

Wednesday
Explore

Take a piece of white card and a glue stick or double-sided tape, and go out into your garden or the local park.

How many different shades of green can you collect? Just take a fingernail-sized corner of each one and arrange them in a way that demonstrates how many greens there really are.

If you're feeling creative you can cover your piece of decorated card with sticky-backed plastic and use it as a bookmark. And next time you're tempted to describe something as 'green', remember how extravagant nature really is.

Thursday
Give
Ever noticed how the letters pages in local papers are full of complaints and criticism? Cheer up 100,000 of your neighbors in a single stroke by composing a letter of praise or recommendation for something locally.

Friday
Expand
Some people do it without a second thought, but most of us cringe at the prospect of haggling over the price tag.

Today, put another dent in your comfort zone by haggling, or at least asking someone to reduce the price of something for you.

After all, there are plenty of cultures where it's *not haggling* that's considered rude. To-ing and fro-ing over the price is an important – and often fun – part of the whole transaction.

Saturday
Receive
Pack a proper old-fashioned picnic today, with sandwiches, fizzy pop, chocolate biscuits, boiled eggs, and a tablecloth. Now find a beauty spot where you can while away a happy hour. Take a storybook with you if you like.

Sunday
Commit
If you sometimes struggle to see pictures in your mind today's your chance to try out another visualization technique which can be just as effective.

Take a piece of paper and some crayons or felt pens and draw your ideal future, a picture representing where you want to be, how you want your life to look and feel. And don't forget to draw yourself into your picture.

I still have the picture I sketched five years ago, showing me writing books at a desk in a window, looking out over a lake. I drew it, then put it away and forgot about it. A year later, we were unexpectedly moving house and as I viewed the room that would be my office I looked at the desk-sized bay window and remembered my picture. It was perfect, apart from the missing lake. The woman selling the house followed my gaze. "You know the best thing about this spot is that when autumn comes and the leaves drop you can see right across to the nature reserve and the lakes." Not one lake but four.

Somehow putting my dreams onto paper had set a ball rolling and now the magic was happening. As you're sketching and coloring, have faith that visualization can bring *your* dreams closer too.

Week 34

date....................

Monday
Explore

A lovely way to waken and invigorate your body is to give it a rubdown. Remember when you were a child, coming out of the sea into a vast towel and being rubbed until your skin tingled pink?

Today I want you to recreate that wonderful alive sensation. Find your softest towel or, alternatively, a soft brush or cloth, and give yourself a body rub all over.

Tuesday
Receive

Go to bed an hour earlier tonight. Once we become grown-ups it's the going to bed early rather than staying up late that is the real treat.

Wednesday
Connect

"Difficult times have helped me understand better than before how infinitely rich and beautiful life is in every way, and that so many things that one goes worrying about are of no importance whatsoever." Isak Dinesen

Imagine you were facing a really difficult time: how many of the things you are worrying about today would still look important?

Thursday
Expand

Play a (kind) practical joke on someone today. No one will be expecting it from *you*.

Friday
Grow

Fake it until you make it is good advice in a world that's far too busy with itself to take us at anything other than face value.

And that applies to our self-esteem too. Today, fake it, by acting as if your self-esteem is already sky high.

Remember the last costume party you went to and how you felt freer, more alive, and more able to be the person you aspire to be by pretending to be someone else?

It's the same idea: dressed in your imaginary coat of healthy self-esteem, walk tall, speak up for yourself and take your place in the world without any apologies.

See how it feels to play the part. Who knows, there might even come a moment when you realize you're no longer faking...

Saturday
Give

Make a greetings card to send to someone special. It means so much more when we gift our time and attention rather than our money.

Sunday
Commit

Meditation doesn't always have to take place in a quiet room, away from the world. If you've ever wondered why anyone might want to spend their nights sitting on a river bank with a fishing rod, or their afternoon on the golf course, it's because we can achieve many of the same benefits of meditation through activities that wholly absorb us.

Cross-stitching, jigsaw puzzles, even the ironing are all everyday meditative practices that people use to quiet their monkey minds and tune into themselves.

Today, choose one activity to be absorbed by. Instead of simply getting on with it, turn it into an act of meditation.

Week 35

date....................

Monday
Receive

There are so many ways in which we're surrounded by news, images and stories designed to worry, depress or simply deaden us.

Today, draw up a list of your favorite feel-good films; a minimum of three, but more if you like. Perhaps they inspire you and remind you of what is possible. Perhaps they have a message about the transforming power of love or self-belief. Or maybe they're just full of wonderful characters you'd love to get to know.

Resolve to view them all again soon, and choose one from your list to watch this week.

Tuesday
Expand

Have you ever noticed how, when you're browsing in a bookshop, the book that you really need to read next seems to jump out at you from the shelf?

Today, there's no need to leave home for a sign. Start by deciding what sort of guidance you need. What's troubling you? Where are you stuck? What are the ways in which you want to grow?

Now head to your own bookshelf and take out the book that seems to announce itself to you. Hold it between your hands for a few moments, then flick the pages and see where they want to fall open.

Is there a message there for you? Sometimes the lesson or the answer is right at hand, just waiting for us to ask.

Wednesday
Give

We may be addicted to email and texting but nothing beats a surprise package in the post. Whether you choose to cut out and send an interesting article, gift a lace handkerchief, or part with a few photographs, pop a surprise in the post for someone today.

Thursday
Connect

Something to think about: if a doctor told you that *your life depended* on you treating yourself better, what would you do differently?

Write down your thoughts, your list of lifesavers, in your journal.

What are you waiting for? Your life *does* depend on it.

Friday
Grow

One of the ways in which low self-esteem shows up in our lives is in what we're willing to put up with.

Somehow we don't really believe we *are* 'worth it'.

Actually, we are. And that means choosing not to put up with the things that constantly reinforce that old, limiting belief: *I don't deserve better.*

Let's start today with what's under your nose, the things you're *putting up with* in your home environment: that squeaky door that puts your teeth on edge, the picture hook that keeps falling off the wall, a wonky lampshade, curtains that don't keep out the light so you wake when the sun does.

Take a tour of your home and make a list of the things that are broken, no longer fit for purpose, or that bother you every time you look at them.

Don't be intimidated if it turns out to be a long list. I'm not asking you to tackle them all right away. Just choose one small niggle to fix this week and then stick the list up on a board where it'll catch your eye from time to time and inspire you to tackle another item.

Saturday
Explore
Whatever tasks you need to do at home today – dishwashing, straightening beds, hanging clothes – choose one to do with a book on your head.

Yes, I know it's a tall order, but that's the point. How often do you stand straight and move with poise and grace? Poise is precisely what all those so-called finishing schools were trying to teach when they set students walking back and forth for hours with books on *their* heads.

Carrying a book reminds us to stand tall and inhabit every inch of our bodies.

Sunday
Commit
Living mindfully means minding our feelings too, for there is no better guide to how well we're doing and what's going on in our heads.

When we're feeling good it's a sure sign that, whatever the difficulties, we are getting closer to the life we want, living authentically.

When we're feeling out of sorts, it's a message from our souls that something is amiss; we are off-course.

Yet, as we've seen, most of us are taught from an early age to hide our feelings rather than show them, even to ourselves.

Today, learn how to use this quick exercise to check in with your feelings, your personal guidance system.

- First, whenever you become aware that your feelings are whispering to you, identify the 'headline'. In her book

Finding Your North Star Martha Beck suggests every feeling is based on one of four headline themes: are you mainly **scared, mad, sad** or **glad**?

- Next, home in a little on that headline by thinking of three or four more words to describe the feeling inside.
- Now, quietly ask yourself why you are feeling the way you are, and wait for your soul to answer.
- Decide whether and how you need to respond.

Week 36
date....................

Monday
Explore

Make today awesome by going in search of awe. Perhaps it's the solidity of an ancient tree, its branches reaching for the heavens. Maybe you're moved by the high cathedral of an endless sky, the vision of those who conceived and constructed a beautiful building, the soft shape of the hills or a seascape, or the bright, curious eyes of a child.

Prepare to be awed wherever you go and whatever you do. See how miraculous this world really is.

Tuesday
Connect

Something to think about today:

If you *absolutely knew* that you couldn't fail, what would you choose to do?

Remember, the real failure may be in not taking a risk at all.

Wednesday
Give

Remember Melly in *Gone With The Wind* donating her wedding ring to raise funds to support the cause her husband was fighting for? There is such power in grand gestures like this when they come from the heart.

Is there something that means a great deal to you that you could part with in order to support a cause close to the heart of a loved one? Or something that has meant a lot to you that you could pass onto someone you love?

Thursday
Grow
Last week we looked at what you're putting up with at home. This week I want you to do an audit of the home that your soul lives in: what are you putting up with in your **diet**, your **fitness**, your **appearance** and your body's **health** in general?

Do you only allow yourself a snatched sandwich at your desk for lunch, leave it three months too long to get a haircut? Do you get out of breath when you have to run for the bus, or put up with a wardrobe full of clothes that don't inspire you one bit?

Don't scare yourself by making a long list. Just choose one thing you're putting up with in each of those four areas.

Resolve to begin to tackle one item this week, even if it's only taking yourself for a walk around the block at lunchtime or making a doctor's appointment about a health niggle that's been bothering you for a while.

Friday
Receive
Often when the weekend arrives we head straight for the security of home and hearth – and another set of responsibilities and things to do. Today, treat yourself to a proper transition. Instead of racing from one life to the other, take time out to celebrate the weekend's arrival. For instance, you could find a peaceful corner of a pub garden for half an hour, take a book to a coffee shop, go for a walk in the park, call on a friend with a bottle of something.

Whatever you choose, remind yourself that every moment of our lives is rich with the possibility of simple pleasures that we forget to make time for, when time is all there is.

Saturday
Expand
Visit an art gallery or, if that's difficult, a shop selling art, or a

library or public building with art on its walls. Choose a piece to sit with for 10–15 minutes, simply studying the artwork, observing your emotional response to it, and noting any thoughts it triggers.

Sunday
Commit

In your life story write about:

- something in your life you wish you'd done
- something you wish you hadn't done, and
- something you wish you'd done differently.

Are there any patterns that emerge; any lessons in these memories for you?

Week 37

date....................

Monday
Commit

My favorite fridge magnet used to read 'Oh no! Not another learning experience'.

It's true, even when it seems impossible that there could be anything positive about the situation we're in, at some level we're learning and growing through it.

So now's the time to learn to look for the silver lining.

Make a list in your journal of some of your blackest moments and then, considering each in turn, work through identifying *at least* one positive: perhaps you learned something, perhaps the experience or event changed you in an important way, perhaps it forced you to do something differently, sent you in a different direction, brought something or someone new into your life.

Looking for the silver lining isn't about denying the pain, hurt, discomfort or despair we may have gone through. It *is* about shining a healing light on what happened and choosing to replace those painful memories with thoughts that strengthen us and bring us peace.

Tuesday
Connect

"There is no way to happiness. Happiness is the way." Wayne Dyer

Instead of waiting for everything to be right so you can be happy, try feeling happy first. And watch how feeling happy makes everything right.

Wednesday
Receive

Play the song 'My Favorite Things' from *The Sound of Music* and substitute the words with your favorite things. You can leave in the "whiskers on kittens" if you like.

Thursday
Expand

Make up your own recipe today instead of consulting the cookbook or sticking to the tried and tested. Be as adventurous as you dare, mixing some of the things in your cupboard, jotting down what you're using as you go. That way, when your dish is a soar-away success, you'll be able to share the recipe with others.

Friday
Give

Instead of looking for signs today, leave one for someone else. On a postcard, write down a favorite quote or a pearl of wisdom that you live by. Leave the card somewhere – to be picked up by someone for whom it will undoubtedly be the perfect message at this time.

Saturday
Grow

As we move into the last quarter of this year of discovery, it's time to focus in on some key questions – such as to what extent are you living your priorities?

It's so easy to keep postponing our priorities for the sake of the day to day. To spend our lives reacting rather than proactively making the changes we need to live a life that reflects the things that truly matter to us.

Today, I want you to imagine that Douglas Adams got it right in *The Hitchhiker's Guide to the Galaxy* and planet Earth really is going to be demolished to make way for a hyperspace bypass.

You've just been given five years' notice that Planet Earth's days are numbered:

- with five years left to live, what would you change?
- what would you put more energy into? And what less?
- what would it be important to make more time for?
- are there any goals or experiences that you'd absolutely get on with and make happen?

Jot down your thoughts in your journal and, when you're done, take a moment to review your list and consider how close, or far removed, it is from how you're living now. Would someone looking at your life right now know what your priorities are?

Sunday
Explore
Give your feet a workout and a treat by going barefoot for as much of today as possible. And be sure to seek out as many different surfaces as you can: soft grass, cool paving slabs, smooth wood, thick carpet.

Week 38

date...................

Monday
Explore

This evening, go and experience the outdoors at dusk. Take a blanket to wrap around you if it's cool and find somewhere to sit and watch and listen as the world settles down for sleep at the end of one more day. It's amazing how every day follows the same pattern, and yet is totally unique.

Tuesday
Grow

Still on the theme of priorities, a crucial part of living our priorities is to understand the difference between what's urgent and what's important, and to shape our lives, as far as we can, around the latter.

So thinking about the next 24 hours, or the week ahead if you prefer a longer timeframe, write two lists:

- what's important
- what's urgent

Write down everything you can think of, and if something is both urgent and important make sure it appears in both lists.

Now, look at the urgent list. If there are any items there that don't also appear on the important list ask yourself why are they there at all?

Other people have a way of hijacking our priorities. Next time you're rushed off your feet or feeling stressed redo this exercise to bring yourself back to what counts.

Wednesday
Expand
Overcome your reluctance to appreciate yourself by starting a self-esteem booster book.

Spend some time writing down any of the compliments or praise you can remember getting. And from now on, whenever someone says something positive about you add it to your book for a handy 'pick-me-up' on those days when you're feeling fragile.

Thursday
Commit
Returning to the theme of living our priorities, today do an audit of how you spend your energy.

- Draw a line down the middle of a page in your journal and on one side list all the activities in your life that energize you, that absorb you so much that you lose track of time, that you love and that bring you alive.
- Now, in the second column, write a list of those activities that drain and deplete you, that you anticipate with a heavy heart, or that you do on automatic.
- What does this show you about the balance of your life?
- In order to shift the balance a little more in your favor decide how you will do more of one of the things that brings you alive and less of one of those that drains you.

Friday
Give
Get a couple of colorful cards and on them write 'thank you for brightening my day'. Tuck them into your bag to hand out when you get the opportunity to instantly acknowledge a kindness someone's done for you.

Saturday
Receive
Today, treat yourself to a new item of attractive underwear. Leave it out to wear tomorrow for no other reason than it'll make you feel good, and feeling good is the key to so much more.

Sunday
Connect
"You do not have to be good", insists Mary Oliver in her poem, *Wild Geese*.

Make that your mantra today as an antidote to a lifetime spent trying to be good.

Actually, you only have to be you.

Week 39

date.....................

Monday
Give
Tell your boss and your colleagues what you appreciate about them today. If you're not working, tell your nearest and dearest why you think they're great.

Tuesday
Connect
"Come to the edge", he said.
    They said, "We are afraid".
    "Come to the edge," he said.
    They came.
    He pushed them... and they flew.
    Guillaume Apollinaire
    Today, identify one area in your life where you are afraid to take a step off the edge. And imagine how wonderful it will be when you find the courage to step... and discover you're flying.

Wednesday
Receive
Write a list of your favorite words today: the words you enjoy saying and hearing, or that lift, inspire or amuse you.

A few of my favorites for starters: peace, quench, love, gossamer, pippin, azure, serene, tickle!

Try and work some of your favorites into your conversations today.

Thursday
Expand
Drive, walk or bus to work by a different route. Enjoy the change of scene.

Friday
Grow

Another way of assessing whether we're living our priorities is to draw a time cake.

First, draw a cake shape. Next, imagine this cake represents your ideal life. Using a colored pen, cut up the slices according to the amount of *waking* time you'd like to be spending on each key area of your life. The sort of categories you might choose are:

- Work outside the house
- Work inside the house
- Being with or talking with friends
- Family time
- Hobbies and interests
- Spiritual practice
- Entertainments
- Health and fitness

Now, imagine this is a typical week in your life and use a different color to shade in how much time you devote to each area in reality.

Do the two look reasonably similar? Or are you definitely not having your cake and eating it?

Saturday
Explore

Today take some paper and crayons out to the garden or park and make your own artwork from bark or leaf rubbings. If you never did this as a child simply lay the paper up against a tree trunk and rub lightly with the side of the crayon. Move on and overlay other sections of tree trunk on top using a different color. Or choose a few interesting-shaped leaves, find a hard spot on the ground and, laying your paper over them, rub to reveal their edges.

Sunday
Commit

So what's *your* personal *Groundhog Day*? You know, the situation that keeps arising, as though someone has pressed the repeat button on your life.

Life has a way of handing out the same lesson over and over again until we finally decide to learn from it and alter our behavior or thinking.

Today, ask yourself what are the situations, the issues, the challenges that just seem to keep coming back at you, over and over again? It might be something as small as always allowing something to run out before you think about replacing it. Or as significant as repeating behaviors that cause you pain, getting into the same row about the same stuff with someone close to you and reacting the same way that you always do.

What is the lesson you need to learn in order to shift the logjam and move on?

Week 40

date....................

Monday
Commit

In your life story describe an event that changed your life or your outlook and explain why it was so significant.

Tuesday
Expand

What do you see when you look in the mirror? The things that are 'wrong': the lines and small blemishes; the odd grey hair; the tired eyes; the nose you wish was smaller? Stop right there! Today adopt a different view and look beyond your looks.

Go somewhere private and spend a couple of minutes *really* seeing yourself in the mirror: not how you look but who you are.

Just this once refuse to be critical. Refuse to focus on what you believe is wrong and instead allow yourself to feel love, compassion and appreciation for the dear person staring back at you.

Wednesday
Grow

We call time to ourselves 'leisure time' but for many of us it would be more accurate to describe it as 'lost time'. Instead of spending it on things we love we've got into the habit of frittering it away on things that don't deliver anything back.

Did you know that research shows shopping and TV-watching account for more of our leisure time than any other activities? But how much of the time you spend doing those things are you consciously enjoying yourself and getting something out of it?

Today, do an audit of lost time in your life. This isn't about making yourself busier but about actively choosing to make your leisure time count. What are the ways in which you could be more alive in those leisure hours, whether you choose to spend them spread out on the sofa or learning to speak Swahili?

Thursday
Connect
"Men stumble over the truth from time to time, but most pick themselves up and hurry off as if nothing happened." Winston Churchill

What truths are you still avoiding?

Friday
Explore
Today, splash your face in the dew. You may have to grit your teeth if it's a cold morning, but tell yourself washing in the dew is supposed to make you even more gorgeous than you already are.

Saturday
Give
Support someone else in their dreams. Find a book signing to attend: not a celebrity one but someone local who's just had their first book published. Or visit an exhibition of photographs or art by a first-timer and tell them you appreciate their work.

Sunday
Receive
Get yourself a large jigsaw puzzle. (Charity shops and boot sales are great sources, but perhaps there's already one stuffed in the back of a cupboard?)

Set it up where you can leave it out for a week or two, coming back to it for a few minutes whenever you're passing and adding a piece or two. Doing a jigsaw puzzle requires full concentration which is the perfect way to quiet your monkey mind in the middle of a busy day.

Week 41

date...................

Monday
Connect
"The remedy for wrongs is to forget them." Publilius Syrus

Have you been practicing forgiveness lately?

Tuesday
Receive
According to some experts, many of us are suffering from dehydration most of the time, living in heated homes and working in air conditioned offices where we're breathing dry air.

Today, hydrate your cells thoroughly by drinking a cool, clear glass of water every hour or two, visualizing it flushing and energizing your whole system. Make it a habit from now on.

Wednesday
Give
Is there someone you've lost touch with? As we grow and change it's natural that the people we want to spend time with change too. But sometimes it's our preoccupation with our own lives that causes us to drift apart.

Take a look at your address book and ask yourself whether there's someone you regret losing touch with. Write them a short note, bringing them up to date and asking how they are.

Whether or not you become close again, it's lovely to let people know you think of them from time to time.

Thursday
Explore
Put a message in a bottle and throw it in the nearest river or lake. You could make the message something fun (like 'please recycle this bottle!'), something personal to do with your hopes for your

own life in the next year, or send special good luck to whoever finds it.

Friday
Expand

When was the last time you went to the theater? For most of us it's a rare treat but there are performances happening all the time in our communities, put on by people who are following their passion. Be brave and check your local paper, library or arts center for an amateur performance to attend. Going along will not only expand you, you'll also be supporting others in their growth.

Saturday
Grow

Now you know more about your true priorities it's time to look at your values. When our lives reflect our deepest values then we are at our most authentic. When the lives we're living force us to compromise our values, we're always likely to feel dissatisfied: strangers to ourselves.

To begin understanding what your values are answer the following questions in your journal:

- Think of two or three people you really admire. For each, what are the qualities that you admire?
- Now, what are the qualities *in you* that you want people to notice? How would you like to be described?

The things you've written down are some of your key values, so now spend a little time considering to what extent are you able to express those values in the way you live now:

- At work
- At home

150

- In your relationships
- In your community
- In your interests and hobbies

What changes could you make in order to move your life closer to your values, to create a life that truly reflects those values?

Sunday
Commit
Some people call them treasure maps, others vision boards: a collage of pictures, quotations, symbols and other stuff that represent what you want to create in your life.

Vision boards are another way of working with visualization and the law of attraction. As you work on your board, and keep it in view; you're again focusing your subconscious mind on moving you in the direction of your hopes and dreams, a bit like a sat nav guiding you in.

There are many wonderful stories of how using a vision board has worked magic in people's lives. I recently came across one I made more than a decade ago and was thrilled to realize that one of the largest pictures on it, of a lake with mountains behind, was the exact scene I'd recently visited with my sister.

Today, make a start on your own board by either finding a large piece of card to stick your images on, buying a scrapbook to use, or hanging up a notice or corkboard where you can see and enjoy it often.

Begin collecting a pile of catalogues or magazines and choose just a couple of images that represent what you want to create in your life to get started with.

Week 42

date....................

Monday
Receive

The writer Cheryl Richardson has a lovely expression to describe how we need to look after ourselves: extreme self-care.

Today, go to extremes in caring for yourself. Linger longer in the shower, remember to lavish cream on your hands after they've been in hot water, eat only nourishing foods, brush your hair 100 times, refuse to get stressed.

You get the idea.

Now how about doing it all over again tomorrow?

Tuesday
Commit

Drop into a travel agent's today and collect a couple of brochures. Now cannibalize them for your vision board, sticking up inspiring pictures of all the places you want to go.

Wednesday
Grow

Last week we looked at values. Today, choose just one of the values on your list: love, compassion, hope, kindness, fun, respect – your decision. Now, whatever you've chosen, your task is to consciously live that value all day long.

Make sure your words, your actions, your body language and your thoughts express that value wherever you are and whatever you're doing. Experience how it feels to truly align with one of your values; to be authentic.

Thursday
Expand

Get your weekly groceries at a different store this week.

Friday
Connect

"Nothing in the outside world needs to change in order for us to feel good." Gill Edwards

Feeling good is an inside job. Go inside today.

Saturday
Give

Have a mini clear-out of a cupboard, drawers or the garden shed. Instead of taking anything in good condition to the charity shop, put it in the street outside with a 'please help yourself' sign. You'll be making someone's day.

Sunday
Explore

Today, create a piece of art from something you find in the natural world.

You could paint a few pebbles, create a mobile from twigs and leaves, work a collage of colors or make a dream catcher threaded with leaves and feathers.

Let your imagination and your creativity run wild. And don't forget to put it somewhere that it can be enjoyed.

Week 43

date....................

Monday
Connect

"No trumpets sound when the important decisions of our lives are made. Destiny is made known silently." Agnes de Mille

Think about the key decisions in your life that were made so silently you scarcely recognized their significance at the time. Are you quietly making any decisions right now?

Tuesday
Grow

A useful exercise for helping to reveal what the life of your dreams might look like is to imagine you've won the lottery. Right now set down in your journal precisely what you would do, what you would have and what you would change if you suddenly won an astonishing amount of money. Make this fun and let your imagination run riot for as long as it wants.

Now we come to the most important part of the exercise: go back over your list and ask yourself which of the things on your list you want to commit to making happen anyway, without waiting for the big cheque.

Often, when we consider what we want, we discover we're using lack of funds as an excuse. Be honest: how many of things you've written down really *do* depend on that windfall? And how many are you holding back on through fear, lack of self-belief, or even lack of desire?

The difference between those who have dreams and those who are living their dreams is more often found in the mind than in the bank.

Wednesday
Explore

You can't beat the smell and taste of fresh herbs. Buy a packet of herb seeds today – basil or coriander are perfect for the kitchen – and plant them in a pot at the sink where you can smell them, watch them grow, and be inspired to include them in the dishes you're cooking.

Thursday
Receive

Treat yourself today by heading to your local craft store to choose a crafting project for the next rainy day.

Friday
Give

Bake some cookies and leave them out on a plate for the refuse collectors by way of appreciation.

Saturday
Expand

At the shops, try on something you would never wear: the boldest, bravest, most unlikely or outrageous outfit you can find. Take your time looking at your reflection in the mirror and asking yourself who you would be if you wore these clothes for real? How would your life be different? What attracted you to those clothes?

Sunday
Commit

Have you heard of the 80/20 rule – otherwise known as the Pareto Principle? It says that 80 percent of our happiness, success and fulfillment comes from 20 percent of the things we do. Which means we spend 80 percent of our time, effort and energy on things that contribute only 20 percent to our overall well-being.

Spend a little time today writing in your journal about which bits of your life belong in the 20 percent that yield the most important results, and which belong in the 80 percent.

Are you satisfied with only 20 percent?

What changes would you need to make to live a 30, 40 or even a 100 percent life?

Week 44

date....................

Monday
Explore

Body language is how we speak without even opening our mouths, so what's yours saying to the people you live with, work with, socialize with and meet on the street?

Very often, we may say one thing with words, but be communicating something entirely different with our bodies.

As you go through today, be aware of what your body is saying. Is it saying interest, energy, aliveness, joy, pleasure, love, confidence? Or the opposite? Are there times when your body's message is fear, reluctance, apology, disinterest or carelessness?

And as you study your body language remember it's not only what you're communicating to others that matters, but what you're saying to yourself. The language of our bodies reflects and reinforces the thoughts and beliefs circulating in our minds as surely as the words coming from our mouths.

Tuesday
Grow

Your imagination has no limits so today in your journal describe the most perfect day you can imagine; from the moment you wake, describe where you are and how you feel, how you spend your day, who you spend it with.

Don't censor yourself in any way. Just for this day you can be anywhere, do anything. Even the sky is not your limit.

What can you discover from what you've written down?

Wednesday
Give

Think of two ways in which you could be kinder to the planet: turn the heating down one degree, use the brake and accelerator pedals on your car less, choose a green product in place of the chemical-laden alternative. Now commit to those two actions from here on.

Thursday
Expand

Change your point of view. When you relax tonight, do so in a different chair, not the one that's become such a fixture that you can still see your shape in it even when you're not there.

Friday
Connect

"Write it on your heart that every day is the best day in the year." Ralph Waldo Emerson

When you choose to make it so, every day can be your best. Make this day count.

Saturday
Commit

"Be still and know that every answer you seek lies inside of you."

Sometimes we are so busy getting on with life we forget to listen to the wisdom of our hearts and souls. Yet so much of what we need to know is already within us, drowned out by the noise of life on the go.

In your journal try out this simple but immensely powerful exercise that allows us to access our inner wisdom, adapted from Lesley Garner's excellent book *Everything I've Ever Done That Worked*.

- Before you begin, allow yourself to sit in quiet meditation for a few minutes.
- Now start a letter beginning **Dear higher self/God/spirit/universe** (whichever you're most comfortable with).

- Without thinking about it too much, write just a few lines describing a situation, problem or issue you'd like help with. Sign it 'yours gratefully' with your name.
- Now, without stopping to think, write your reply straight back:
- Dear (your name)
- This is how I see your situation...
- This is what I think you should do...
- Don't try and think about this too much and don't censor what is appearing on the page. Just allow the words to flow. Often this exercise produces some wonderful insights.
- At some level, you already know the answer.

Sunday
Receive

Today, get out the playing cards or a board game and persuade someone to have a game with you. Rediscover one of life's simplest pleasures.

Week 45
date....................

Monday
Receive
Turn a cup of tea into a special treat by making a ceremony of it. That means instead of dunking a tea bag in a mug you set out tea leaves, real milk in a jug and your best china.

Warm the pot, leave the tea to draw, pour it through a strainer and add a splash of milk to the clear liquid. If you take sugar, use lumps, and tongs to put them into your cup.

Enjoy all of this consciously, from the sounds of the chinking china and trickling liquid, to taking small sips from a bone china cup, rolling the flavor around on your tongue.

Tuesday
Connect
Something to think about:

"Life isn't about finding yourself. Life is about creating yourself." George Bernard Shaw

Are you happy with the way your creation is taking shape?

Wednesday
Grow
We all have responsibilities, to our families and friends, our communities, the wider world, and to ourselves. But we're inclined to forget, in our effort to be good people, that we also have rights. So today, write your own personal bill of rights, for instance:

- I have the right to be treated with respect
- I have the right to be myself, no matter how others would like me to be
- I have the right to my dreams

Go on – really think about what you have a right to, and as you do so make a vow to honor your rights from now on.

Thursday
Give

Leave flowers and a message of love at a war memorial today.

Friday
Explore

Have you added anything to your nature corner lately? The year has moved on, and it's time to take a wander down the garden or through the park to discover a few more things that bring you pleasure when you look at them. A nature table needs to be a dynamic thing; not a museum.

Saturday
Commit

Collect a few store catalogues next time you're at the shops and schedule in another session cutting out pictures to stick onto your vision board.

Now it's really beginning to take shape, be sure to hang it somewhere that you will often see it and can enjoy thinking about all the wonderful things on it.

Remind yourself to go on dreaming, cutting and sticking, and every so often to review what's up there, add new material and take away those of your dreams that have now turned up.

Sunday
Expand

Last week, you changed your seat to change your viewpoint. This week, try moving a few pieces of furniture around, or swap the pictures on the walls.

We get so used to our environment we forget we can change it. It's amazing how even small shifts can have an energizing effect.

Week 46

date...................

Monday
Expand

Choose a piece of classical music and spend five minutes really listening, noticing its complexity and mood, following the sounds of the different instruments, trying to understand what the composer and musicians are communicating, monitoring your own emotional reaction.

So much of the time we are passive rather than active listeners: no composer ever wrote a piece of music expecting it to be background.

Tuesday
Connect

"Out beyond ideas of wrongdoing and rightdoing,

there is a field. I'll meet you there," wrote the Persian poet Rumi.

Whose rules are you living by and how well do they serve you?

Wednesday
Commit

In your life story write about a time when you were embarrassed. Why? What caused you to be embarrassed and what, if anything, did you do about it?

What embarrasses you now? What do you need to learn about embarrassment?

Thursday
Explore

Set up a container outside to collect rainwater so you can use it for the final rinse next time you wash your hair. It'll make your hair as soft as down.

Friday
Give
Leave a lottery ticket for a waiter as part of your tip, or pop it under a wiper blade or through someone's door. We never know how our actions may spread like ripples through the lives of others. Most likely you will never know the outcome of this act of kindness, but how wonderful to imagine those numbers coming up for someone who really deserves a break.

Saturday
Receive
Make a set of message cards that you can draw on when you need inspiration, reassurance or direction.

First get some blank cards or plain postcards and onto each card write one of your favorite affirmations, quotes or things to think about from this book. If someone's paid you a nice compliment you could write that down too.

Decorate your cards with inspiring pictures from magazines, or get colored pens and illustrate the cards.

Now whenever you're feeling a little lost or lackluster simply shuffle your deck and draw out one of the cards. It will almost certainly have an important message for you.

Sunday
Grow
As your best year yet draws to a close, ready to give way to an even more wonderful year ahead, it's time to start getting clear about where you're heading, how the life of your dreams looks, your purpose on this planet.

So for starters, today imagine it's your 90th birthday and your family and friends have come together to celebrate your life with a party.

The highlight comes when your best friend stands up to pay tribute to you.

In your journal, write your best friend's speech for them, imagining what you'd like them to be saying about who are you, what you've made of your life, and your legacy to others.

Week 47

date....................

Monday
Connect
Something to think about:

"Just trust yourself, then you will know how to live." Goethe

To what extent do you trust yourself? In which areas of your life do you find it hardest to trust you? Could you trust yourself more on the subject of your own life?

Tuesday
Expand
How many times in your life have you not done something because you were waiting for someone to grant you permission?

Now consider how many of the people you most admire will have waited for permission before getting on and doing the things they dreamed of doing?

We could wait all our lives, but why would we when the only one we really need permission from is ourselves?

Today, identify just one thing you're waiting for permission to do. And do it anyway.

Wednesday
Give
Today, be a shoeshine. Collect every pair of shoes from the bottom of wardrobes and polish/wash/scrub them clean. When we do it for others, shining shoes is a surprisingly meaningful act of service.

Thursday
Grow
Looking back at the 90th birthday party speech you drafted last week, choose just one of the key themes or achievements that

you wrote about that you are ready to begin turning into a reality.

A tried and tested technique that's really effective is to work back from your goal, turning it into a series of small, manageable actions.

- In your journal write the numbers one to ten, with ten being the moment you achieve whichever of your goals you've selected.
- Write that goal in alongside the number ten.
- Now, starting at one, fill in the gaps, identifying the nine steps you can take to get you from where you are to where you want to be. For example, if the birthday speech mentioned how wonderful it was that you achieved your dream of spending six months traveling the world then number ten would be you taking off on your travels. Step nine might be booking the air tickets, step eight negotiating time off work, right back to steps one and two, deciding where you want to go and sticking up the pictures on your vision board, then setting up a savings account and a standing order to pay a set amount into your escape fund each month.

Friday
Explore
Another way in which we can tune into our inner wisdom is by taking our questions and asking for guidance out into the natural world.

- Begin by taking a quiet moment to identify what it is you want to know or want help with.
- Now head outside and find somewhere to sit that you won't be disturbed.
- Remain sitting there in silence for 20 minutes or so, just observing what is around you.

- As you sit, simply open yourself up to the possibility that the natural world around you has a message or an answer for you. Do not try to force this. Just allow what comes.
- At the end, take your journal and jot down anything that comes to mind.

Saturday
Commit

You've been practicing affirmations and visualization to support you in moving towards a more authentic life. Now see how the experts do it!

If you haven't come across it yet, *The Secret* by Rhonda Byrne is one of a number of recent books that describe the law of attraction, how it works and how to use it.

Get hold of a copy of the film of the book, packed with self-help gurus and high-powered positivity.

Put your tongue in your cheek if you must, but I promise you *will* come away feeling inspired, and with lots of practical ideas on using visualization to change *your* life. If you've already seen it, watch it through again.

Sunday
Receive

Treat yourself to a technology-free day today. Believe me, if you leave the computer, the mobile phone, and even the TV, switched off today, you'll not only get more done, you'll also discover you have more time for you.

Week 48

date....................

Monday
Receive

Write down ten ways in which you are better at your current age than you were when you were half your current age (are you with me?)

Tuesday
Grow

Last week you made your action plan for moving towards one of the lifetime goals you've set yourself. If you haven't already done so, get started on step one today – or move to step two if you've already ticked off the first of your nine actions.

Now choose another of the goals that was mentioned in your birthday speech and write a new ten-step action list for that one.

As so many excellent life coaches remind us, we really can get almost anywhere so long as we just keep putting one foot in front of the other. If you're interested in learning more about these success strategies Jack Canfield's *The Success Principles* is one of the most readable, practical and thorough programs I've come across. After all, *a goal is simply a dream on which you're taking action.*

Wednesday
Explore

Revisit another of those forgotten childhood pleasures by grabbing some tidbits and heading off to feed the ducks.

Thursday
Give

Become a tither. Even if you only have a little to give, making a regular donation to charity is a way of demonstrating your gratitude for what you have in your life, and recognizing how abundance needs to flow back and forth.

You can either set up a direct debit to a particular charity or identify a day on each month when you will pop a couple of coins into a charity box.

Friday
Connect
Something to think about today:

"When we are no longer able to change a situation, we are challenged to change ourselves." Viktor Frankl

Are there areas in your life where you are still fighting, still resisting? Instead of taking responsibility for the only bit you can change: your attitude.

Saturday
Expand
Just like having a camera in our hands, holding a paintbrush somehow enables us to see the world differently. Suddenly we're paying attention to the details, to the relationships, and to the beauty.

Today, get some watercolors, a brush and paper and paint what you see from a window, or, if you'd prefer, at a local beauty spot.

It doesn't matter if you 'can't'. No one need see your painting but you.

It doesn't even matter what you put onto the paper, so long as you allow yourself to get absorbed in what you are doing, and leave behind the critical voice that thinks there's no point doing something unless you can do it perfectly.

Sunday
Commit
In your journal, have fun identifying the musical soundtrack of

your life: the top ten tunes that remind you of significant times or people, represent turning points, or that say something about who you were and who you are.

Once you've whittled your list down to just ten tracks, and written a few words about why each of those tunes has earned its place in the musical of your life, you could save all ten to a special 'my life in music' folder on your MP3.

Week 49

date...................

Monday
Commit

Decisions, decisions. So often we see decision-making as a challenge, and come at it with our minds fixed on damage limitation: making the choice that involves the least risk.

But decisions are a chance to shape our lives and our future, packed with possibilities. As usual, it comes down to how we choose to think about them.

The following techniques are useful to guide you whenever you're facing a decision. Try them out now on something you currently need to make a decision on:

- *On the horns of a dilemma:* only two choices and you've got a dilemma; three or more and you have a choice. So invest time in coming up with as many possible options as you can.
- *Get focused:* the longer we worry about a decision, the more variables we load onto it. In among all the what-ifs there's usually one factor that's the most important. Concentrate on that – everything else is details.
- *Make believe:* try pretending that you've already made the decision and over the next few hours monitor your feelings. Relief, peace – if it feels good, even though it's scary, then go ahead. Edginess, justification, unease are all signals you need to test out another of the possible choices.
- *A stomach for decision-making:* according to house agents the average time it takes people to decide about something as major as buying a new home is just ten minutes. That's because it's one area where people are happy to follow their gut instinct. What does your gut tell you about the decision you're facing?

- *No bad decisions:* instead of worrying about bad decisions remind yourself that every decision represents movement in our lives, and movement is how we learn and grow.

Tuesday
Connect
At the start of the year (p. 14) I asked you to identify what questions this year was asking of you. As we approach year-end, look back at what you wrote in your journal then.

Take a few deep breaths and ask yourself whether you now have any answers. Take a pen and let your subconscious do the talking by setting down whatever comes to mind as you ponder what you wrote then.

Wednesday
Receive
Add a touch of sparkle to your life: buy yourself something glittery to hang on your walls, your front door, or on you.

Thursday
Grow
We're going back to goal-setting for one final time this week, to help you really establish a healthy new habit of taking small, inspired actions in pursuit of your dreams.

Amazingly, one of the main reasons most of us haven't already achieved our dreams in life is because we gave up too quickly – or never even started.

So this week, move onto the next step in your action ladder on both of the goals you identified to work on.

If those actions represent more than can be achieved in a single week then put a time and date against the next step, identifying when you plan to achieve it by. And write some notes on what you need to do to get you there.

Don't ever think the steps you're taking are too small. And

don't allow yourself to worry about how long it might take. Remember that the journey matters every bit as much as the destination if you travel hopefully and positively and *never forget that now is the most important time of all.*

Friday
Explore
Now you've begun to aim for the stars, let's get some inspiration from them.

Tonight, or any time this week when the sky is clear, spend a few minutes being a stargazer.

If it's warm you might like to lie down on a rug, staring upwards. If it's chilly, why not take your cocoa out with you?

Whatever the weather, notice how impossibly huge our universe is, how many millions of pinpricks of light make up the glittering canopy over our heads.

How perfect it is.

Saturday
Give
Today, cheer up people you will never meet by finding an imaginative way to leave a message of love, peace, joy or good humor for whoever happens to be passing. One of the greeting cards I love to send features the word 'love' spelt out in large pebbles on a cliff top.

How could you leave a message to surprise others?

Sunday
Expand
Print off a map of the world from the Internet or tear the pages from a world atlas. Now stick a colored pin in all the places you've been.

Choose a different color and stick pins in all those places you intend to go.

Week 50

date....................

Monday
Receive

Whatever the time of year, choose a seasonal treat for yourself today. If it's summer, how about strawberries and cream, or asparagus in butter? My winter favorite is gingerbread latte, which always lets me know Christmas is coming. You can make it at home by stirring ginger syrup into milky coffee and topping it with whipped cream and a sprinkle of cinnamon. Heaven in a cup!

Tuesday
Commit

Look at the reading list at the back of this book, and at the back of any books and materials you may have acquired along the way. Write out your own reading list for the year ahead and go ahead and order the first couple of titles from either the local library or a bookstore. If Christmas or a birthday is coming up, add the books to your wish list.

Wednesday
Grow

Have you seen those columns in the weekend newspapers, where celebrities tell us what they've learned about life?

Have fun doing your own 'This much I know' column today: the truths you've learned as you go through life that you would like to share with others.

A sentence on each one is plenty and they don't all have to be serious. For instance, I know that:

- The to-do list will always be there so I shouldn't beat myself up trying to get to the end of it.

- There is nothing more important than giving and receiving love.
- Chocolate gives me spots, whatever the experts say.
- A solid uninterrupted night's sleep always leaves me feeling a million dollars.

You get the idea: don't stop till you've written at least ten of your truths.

Thursday
Give
Imagine how stressful a shop assistant's life can be, dealing with sometimes difficult members of the public. Today, write a letter of praise to the manager of a shop or service where one or more members of staff were helpful and kind. It will mean even more to them to have your thanks come via their boss – and may even do them some good.

Friday
Connect
Something to think about:
  "Ask and it will be given to you.
  Seek, and you will find.
  Knock, and the door will be opened to you." St Luke's Gospel
  Do you need to have more faith?

Saturday
Expand
Museums, schools, galleries, churches, local societies: so much effort goes into putting an exhibition together, so honor other people's energy today by taking yourself off to a local exhibition, expanding your own horizons at the same time.

Sunday
Explore

Make some decorations for your home by clipping greenery from the hedgerows. Head out with a pair of secateurs and get an armful of greenery that you can weave into wreaths for the door, braid along the mantelpiece and drape on bookshelves and pictures. Quite apart from looking great, natural decorations also make the home smell wonderful.

Week 51

date....................

Monday
Expand
Get up an hour earlier. How does it feel? The quiet morning hours can be such a gift, giving us an opportunity to think, plan, prepare, read, meditate – uninterrupted. Could you give yourself this extra breathing space more often?

Tuesday
Connect
"The best years of your life are the ones in which you decide your problems are your own. You do not blame them on your mother, the ecology, or the president. You realize that you control your own destiny." Albert Ellis

Are you ready for more best years?

Wednesday
Receive
Treat yourself to the most extravagant bath bomb you can find, and turn bath time into spa-time.

Thursday
Give
Learn a joke and tell it to others today in order to put a smile on their faces.

Friday
Commit
One of the most important messages I've wanted to share with you this year is that a rich life is one in which we are truly awake and living consciously.

The daily download (p. 15) is one way of practicing

awareness and, as we reach the end of our year together, here's another that you can use from time to time.

Thinking back over the last year (or month, or week, depending on how you choose to use this tool), complete the following sentences:

- The time I felt most angry was...
- The time I felt most upset was...
- The time I felt most frightened was...
- The time I felt most lonely was...
- The time I felt most loved was...
- The time I felt most powerful was...
- The time I felt most fulfilled was...
- The time I felt most authentic was...

Thinking ahead to the coming year, what can you learn from your answers?

Saturday
Explore
We've looked at the musical soundtrack of your life, but what about the background sounds that are there every moment of our days? Whether it's the thrum of cars racing by, the TV in the background or Muzak at the shops, the experience of true silence is so rare.

Today, find some way of experiencing as near silence as you can. It might mean locking yourself away, or heading out away from roads and airplanes and children's voices.

Silence heals and repairs, sooths, restores and nourishes even the busiest, noisiest soul.

Embrace the silence and let your soul fall into it, experiencing a few moments of profound peace.

Sunday
Grow

Write a message to your future self, five years down the line.

Get your best writing paper and let your thoughts flow. How do you want to encourage yourself, what kind of life will your future self be living and what do you want to say about how you got there? What do you want yourself to have done/seen/achieved five years from now?

Date the letter, seal it in an envelope addressed and dated five years from now. Then tuck it into the cover of a book, hide it in the back of cupboard you only clear every five years, or give it to a friend for safekeeping.

Week 52

date....................

Monday
Expand

We're about to celebrate the end of this wonderful year and the start of an even more amazing new one. So today's a good time to focus on some of the fun, excitement, growth, fulfillment and adventure you are going to enjoy over the next 12 months.

In your journal, complete the following sentences: This new year is the year I am going to:

- Read...
- Visit...
- Try...
- Taste...
- See...
- Hear...
- Tackle...
- Change the way I think about....
- Change the way I do...
- And I am going to...

Tuesday
Explore

Plant something that will not appear above the earth until next year. Express your faith in the endless circle of life.

Wednesday
Grow

We've worked our way through many tools and techniques this year and learned that, using them, we have the power to change.

As you look ahead to the next 12 months, spend a little time looking back over this book and choosing which tools you've found most helpful and want to make a part of your regular practice.

Each day I make time for meditation, reading inspiring books, writing in my journal, physical exercise, affirmations and the daily download. I've learned that when I do so I have a good day.

What do you want to build into each day or each week?

Write your own daily or weekly plan.

Thursday
Give

Take a box of doughnuts into a local health center for the staff to share among themselves.

Friday
Commit

"Today isn't any other day, you know." Lewis Carroll

We've spent this year discovering all the ways in which we can ensure there is no such thing as an ordinary day. No matter how busy we are, how challenged or troubled, we can create at least a few moments that lift us up out of the ordinary.

Thinking of the gift of all those new days, stretching out in front of you, how will you continue to make each day special? To make your minutes count?

Write your own promise to yourself and stick it up where you will see it every day, for instance:

- To spend time with those I love
- To give and receive and appreciate both
- To be as present as I can in my life by taking my time and using all my senses
- To go on growing
- To continue to use the tools in this book I've found helpful
- To remind myself every day that I'm choosing to live the breadth of my life as well as its length.

Saturday
Receive
A lovely ritual to use on significant days such as your birthday, New Year's Eve, and the day you finish this book, is to organize a private celebration.

Lock yourself away somewhere that you won't be disturbed and light only candles to illuminate the room.

Put on your very favorite piece of inspiring music (I use the theme tune to *Out of Africa*), your most comfortable clothes, and pour yourself a drink of something with bubbles in: sparkling wine or juice, your choice.

Allow yourself up to an hour to simply sit, be, reflect on the peace and on what lies behind and ahead. Let each mouthful of bubbles be a toast to the wonderful person you are and all that you are learning, achieving and becoming. Let each soaring note of the music remind you of what a glorious gift this life is.

Sunday
Connect
"There are many great and beautiful arts in the world, but the greatest of all is the art of living.
Go on living beautifully."
Isak Dinesen

Wishing you a lifetime of beautiful days xxx

MOVING ON

Recommended books and other resources

This list of brilliant books, CDs and DVDs is both a bibliography and a recommended reading list for your own future exploring.

Some of the titles are directly referenced in the pages of *Have the Best Year of Your Life*. Others have been such an important part of my own growth and learning I want to share them with you. In most cases, I've referenced the edition I've read, which isn't always the first time the book was published. Some of the titles have also been issued by different publishers in different countries.

Rather than overwhelm you, I have only selected my favorite titles: almost anything by any of the following authors is worth pursuing when you have time. I've also done my best to sort them into categories to help you in following up those areas that most interest you, but do bear in mind many of these resources could equally well be placed in most, if not all of the categories I've chosen.

Foundation Stones

Dawn Breslin, *Dawn Breslin's Guide to Super Confidence* (Hay House, 2006)

Wayne W Dyer and Byron Katie, *Making your Thoughts Work for You* **CD** (Hay House, 2007)

Gill Edwards, *Living Magically* (Piatkus, 1991)

Gill Edwards, *Life is a Gift* (Piatkus, 2007)

Lynn Grabhorn, *Excuse Me, Your Life is Waiting* (Hodder & Stoughton, 2004)

Louise L Hay, *You Can Heal Your Life* (Hay House, 1984)

Louise L Hay, *Heal Your Body* (Hay House, 1988)

Louise L Hay, *You Can Heal Your Life Companion Book* (Hay House, 2002)

Louise L Hay, *The Power is Within You* (Hay House, 1991)

Susan Jeffers, *Feel the Fear and Do It Anyway* (20th anniversary edition, Rider, 2007)

Susan Jeffers, *Feel the Fear and Beyond* (Rider, 1998)

Byron Katie, *Loving What Is* (Harmony, 2002)

Denise Linn, *Soul Coaching* (Hay House, 2003)

Marianne Williamson, *A Return to Love* (Harper, 1996)

Creativity

Julia Cameron, *The Artist's Way* (Pan, 1995)

Julia Cameron, *Walking in this World* (Rider, 2002)

Films

The Shift Dr Wayne W Dyer (Hay House, 2009)

The Secret (2006, TS Production)

What the Bleep Do We Know? (Revolver, 2005)

You Can Heal Your Life (Hay House, 2007)

Happiness

Robert Holden, *Happiness Now* (Hodder & Stoughton, 1998)

Marci Shimoff, *Happy For No Reason* (Simon & Schuster, 2008)

Law of Attraction

Rhonda Byrne, *The Secret* (Atria, 2006)

Patricia Crane, *Ordering from the Cosmic Kitchen* (The Crane's Nest, 2002)

Wayne W Dyer, *You'll See It When You Believe It* (Arrow, 1990)

Wayne W Dyer, *The Power of Intention* (Hay House, 2004)

Esther and Jerry Hicks, *Ask and It Is Given* (Hay House, 2005)

Esther and Jerry Hicks, *The Law of Attraction* (Hay House, 2006)

Florence Scovel-Shinn, *The Game of Life & How to Play It* (Vermilion, 2005)

Life Purpose

Martha Beck, *Finding Your Own North Star* (Piatkus, 2001)

Viktor Frankl, *Man's Search for Meaning* (Beacon, 2006)

Marianne Williamson, *The Age of Miracles* **CD** (Hay House, 2008)

Life Skills

Ingrid Bacci, *The Art of Effortless Living* (Bantam, 2002)

Sarah Ban Breathnach, *Simple Abundance* (Bantam, 1996)

Dawn Breslin, *Affirmations to Change Your Life* **CD** (www.dawnbreslin.com)

David D Burns, *Feeling Good* (Avon, 1999)

Richard Carlson, *Don't Sweat the Small Stuff* (Mobius, 1998)

Lynda Field, *Fast Track to Happiness* (Vermilion, 2006)

Lynda Field, *60 Ways to Heal Your Life* (Element, 1999)

Lesley Garner, *Everything I've Ever Done that Worked* (Hay House, 2004)

Phil Murray, *The Flow of Life* (Hodder & Stoughton, 1999)

Cheryl Richardson, *Take Time for Your Life* (Bantam, 2000)

Stuart Wilde, *Life was Never Meant to be a Struggle* (Hay House, 1987)

Meditation, Visualization and Breathing

Aeoliah, *Angel Love* **CD** (Oreade Music, 1999)

Wayne W Dyer, *Meditations for Manifesting* **CD** (Hay House, 2004)

Shakti Gawain, *Creative Visualization* (New World Library, 2002)

Shakti Gawain, *The Creative Visualization Workbook* (Nataraj, 1995)

Shakti Gawain, *Creative Visualization Meditation* **CD** (New World Library, 2002)

Louise L Hay, *Morning and Evening Meditations* **CD** (Hay House, 1983)

Jenny James, *Sleeping Angels* **CD** (Sounds Wonderful, 2004)

Oriah Mountain Dreamer, *The Invitation* (Thorsons, 1999)

Oriah Mountain Dreamer, *The Call* (Element, 2003)

Andrew Weil, MD, *Breathing: The Master Key to Self Healing* **CD**

(Sounds True, 1999)

Mindfulness

Joanna Field, *A Life of One's Own* (Virago, 1986)

Eckhart Tolle, *The Power of Now* (Hodder & Stoughton, 2001)

Eckhart Tolle, *Living a Life of Inner Peace* **CD** (New World Library, 2004)

Thich Nhat Hanh, *The Miracle of Mindfulness* (Rider, 1991)

New Science

Gregg Braden, *The Spontaneous Healing of Belief* (Hay House, 2008)

Bruce Lipton, *The Biology of Belief* (Cygnus, 2005)

Lynne McTaggart, *The Intention Experiment* (Harper Element, 2007)

Poetry

Mary Oliver, *Wild Geese* (Bloodaxe, 2004)

David Whyte, *Midlife and the Great Unknown* **CD** (Sounds True, 2003)

Signs

Steven D Farmer, *Animal Spirit Guides* (Hay House, 2006)

Denise Linn, *Signposts* (Rider, 1996)

The Spiritual Life

Deepak Chopra, *The Seven Spiritual Laws of Success* (Excel, 1996)

Wayne W Dyer, *There is a Spiritual Solution to Every Problem* (Thorsons, 2001)

Lao-Tzu, *Tao Te Ching* (translated by Stephen Mitchell, Macmillan, 1989)

David Lawrence Preston, *365 Steps to Practical Spirituality* (How To Books, 2007)

Success

Jack Canfield, *The Success Principles* (Element, 2005)

Paul McKenna, *Change Your Life in 7 Days* (Bantam, 2004)

Michael Neill, *You Can Have What You Want* (Hay House, 2007)

BOOKS

O is a symbol of the world, of oneness and unity. In different cultures it also means the "eye," symbolizing knowledge and insight. We aim to publish books that are accessible, constructive and that challenge accepted opinion, both that of academia and the "moral majority."

Our books are available in all good English language bookstores worldwide. If you don't see the book on the shelves ask the bookstore to order it for you, quoting the ISBN number and title. Alternatively you can order online (all major online retail sites carry our titles) or contact the distributor in the relevant country, listed on the copyright page.

See our website www.o-books.net for a full list of over 500 titles, growing by 100 a year.

And tune in to myspiritradio.com for our book review radio show, hosted by June-Elleni Laine, where you can listen to the authors discussing their books.

MySpiritRadio